AIR WAR AGAINST

AIR WAR
AGAINST HITLER'S GERMANY

HITLER'S GERMANY

BY THE EDITORS OF

AMERICAN HERITAGE

The Magazine of History

AUTHOR

STEPHEN W. SEARS

CONSULTANT

MARVIN W. McFARLAND

*Chief, Science and Technology Division,
Library of Congress*

PUBLISHED BY

AMERICAN HERITAGE
PUBLISHING CO., INC.

New York

BOOK TRADE AND INSTITUTIONAL DISTRIBUTION BY

HARPER & ROW

FIFTH PRINTING

© 1964 by American Heritage Publishing Co., Inc., 551 Fifth
Avenue, New York, New York, 10017. All rights reserved under
Berne and Pan-American Copyright Conventions. Library of Con-
gress Catalog Card Number: 64-17357. Trademark AMERICAN
HERITAGE JUNIOR LIBRARY registered United States Patent Office.

Foreword

"This is the day of the airplane and the submarine. In these two forces will be the strength in the next war."

Prophetic words, which were spoken not by an admiral of a nuclear submarine fleet nor by a general of the Strategic Air Command, but by General Billy Mitchell of the youthful American Army Air Service in 1925. Mitchell was looking ahead with penetrating clarity to the war that would follow World War I.

Despite the best efforts of peaceful men, World War II came, pushed by the evil genius of Adolf Hitler. And as Billy Mitchell had foreseen, it was the airplane which gave the Allies a vital weapon for victory. This book tells the story of the American daylight bombing campaign against Nazi Germany. There were other air wars fought in the years 1939–1945 —by Britons against Germans, by Germans against Russians, by Americans against Japanese, among others—but none was more dramatic nor more savage than this one.

The paintings and sketches accompanying the narrative are the work of American, British, and German war artists. Even more graphic are the combat photographs reproduced here. These are not the polished work of professional photographers. Some are from film taken by the automatic cameras mounted in fighter planes; others are quick snapshots taken from bombers in the heat of action, with little thought to composition or proper lighting. But each captures for history a dramatic moment in the fastest-moving of all forms of warfare.

The air war against Hitler's Germany took place only two decades ago, yet every warplane seen or described in this book has long since outlived its military usefulness. In a few short years these totally new weapons were conceived and built, made their fight, and became obsolete. Never again will massed armadas of a thousand or more bombers fight their way through hundreds of enemy fighters to try and destroy centers of war production.

Yet it is worth remembering in this atomic age that in the space of fourteen hours in February, 1945, lumbering propeller-driven bombers, carrying loads of "conventional" bombs, visited upon the German city of Dresden the greatest single man-made calamity in Europe's history. The air war over Europe proved to the world that havoc from the skies could be even more earth-shaking than Billy Mitchell, or any other man, could have dreamed.

—The Editors

U.S. AIR FORCE

An aircraft factory producing German fighter planes is the target of these bombs spilling from the bomb bay of a U.S. Flying Fortress.

FRONT ENDSHEET: *Flying Fortresses
and their high-flying escort fighters
trace vapor trails in the German sky.*
U.S. AIR FORCE

BACK ENDSHEET: *U.S. Liberators
set fires in the huge oil refineries at
Ploesti, Rumania, in a 1944 attack.*
U.S. AIR FORCE

COVER: *The view from a waist gunner's position in a B-17, pictured
by American war artist Peter Hurd.*
TIME-LIFE COLLECTION, DEFENSE DEPARTMENT

TITLE PAGE: *A water color by John
Lavalle shows B-17s of the U.S. Fif-
teenth Air Force over Italy in 1944.*
U.S. AIR FORCE

This patriotic recruiting poster features a flight of B-17s.

Contents

1

MISSION NUMBER 52

Groaning and grumbling, 280 American airmen dragged themselves out of bed in the early morning darkness at a United States Army Air Force heavy bomber base in England. They washed, dressed, ate their usual bland army breakfast, and then assembled in a big Quonset hut to be briefed on their target for the day. The date was April 17, 1943; World War II was in its fourth year.

The commander of the base's bomber group mounted a platform at the end of the hut and quickly ended the suspense. The target of Mission Number 52 (that is, the fifty-second mission to be flown by the U.S. Eighth Air Force) was the big Focke-Wulf aircraft factory at Bremen in northwestern Germany.

Here was a real chance to hit Nazi Germany where it would hurt, the group commander said. The Bremen factory was the leading producer of the Luftwaffe's Focke-Wulf 190, the best fighter plane in the German Air Force. As usual, the bombers would attack by daylight; as usual, in attacking a target so far from England, they would be flying beyond the range of friendly escort fighters. They would be

entirely on their own over Germany.

The commander stepped aside, and his place was taken by the group intelligence officer, who filled in details on the mission and its target. This was to be a maximum effort, he said—four bomber groups, well over 100 planes in all, the Eighth Air Force's biggest raid so far. The Focke-Wulf factory was a juicy target, and the airmen could expect the Luftwaffe to be up in force. Intelligence estimated that at least 100 German fighters were based near the route the bombers would follow to Bremen.

The weatherman came next, predicting cloud and wind conditions to be expected over England and the Continent. Then came the flak officer, warning at what points on the route the heaviest German antiaircraft fire would be found. This officer added his usual remark about flak being only a nuisance. The fliers laughed hollowly. They hated and feared the ugly black shellbursts that knocked down bombers or crippled them so that they

As a mechanic works on the number one engine, other ground crewmen "bomb up" an Eighth Air Force Flying Fortress. A B-17 carried two to three tons of bombs and some eight tons of fuel on the average mission.

The U.S. bomber crewmen above set their watches during a briefing. The projector at center showed reconnaissance photographs of the target. Bombs were fuzed (right) just before takeoff. Fuzes were set for a fraction of a second after impact so that the bombs would go through the roof of a factory and then explode inside.

became easy prey for the enemy's fighters.

After detailed briefings on bombing tactics, navigation, and radio signals, the crews dressed in their flight gear and climbed into trucks to ride out to their planes. The Boeing B-17 Flying Fortresses squatted on paved hardstands around the edge of the airfield, widely separated in case of enemy air attack. Ground crewmen had been at work most of the night loading bombs and ammunition and repairing battle damage from the previous day's raid on well-defended enemy submarine bases along the coast of German-occupied France. The sergeant gunners checked over their .50 caliber machine guns and lifted them into the Fortresses. As the gunners went to work mounting their weapons, the crew officers ran through a detailed preflight check to make sure everything in these complex airplanes was working right.

Bombardiers carefully lifted bombsights into the noses of the B-17s. The Norden bombsight was a vital part of the mission; in the hands of a skilled man this precision computer was supposed to be able to drop a bomb into a pickle barrel from four miles up. That, at any rate, was the theory. Un-

der combat conditions, with German fighters whipping past, exploding flak shells rocking the plane, and the bomber's guns chattering around him, the bombardier had a hard time living up to the pickle-barrel boast.

The bombardiers had another task to perform before their ground duties were finished. They crawled into the yawning bomb bay of each plane and fitted fuzes into the ten 500-pound

FINLAND

NORWAY

SWEDEN

ESTONIA

NORTH SEA

DENMARK

LATVIA

BALTIC SEA

LITHUANIA

IRELAND

Liverpool

Coventry

ENGLAND

London

English Channel

HOLLAND

FRISIAN ISLANDS

Wilhelmshaven

Danzig

Vegesack

Hamburg

Bremen

Berlin

Münster

POLAND

Dortmund

Magdeburg

Essen

Oschersleben

BELGIUM

Lille

Kassel

Merseburg

Dresden

Cologne

Rouen

Frankfurt

Marienburg

Paris

Schweinfurt

Seine River

Loire River

Nuremburg

CZECHOSLOVAKIA

Rhine River

Regensburg

Danube

*ATLANTIC
OCEAN*

Rhône River

Munich

Vienna

HUNGARY

SWITZERLAND

AUSTRIA

Wiener Neustadt

FRANCE

RUMANIA

River

SPAIN

YUGOSLAVIA

ITALY

*ADRIATIC
SEA*

CORSICA

Rome

ALBANIA

SARDINIA

GREECE

SICILY

ALGERIA

MALTA

TUNISIA

MEDITERRANEAN SEA

TARGET GERMANY

*Cities and Installations Hit by Allied bombers,
1941-1945*

LIBYA

Benghazi

ALLIED COUNTRIES

GERMANY

AXIS-OCCUPIED COUNTRIES

NEUTRAL COUNTRIES

✈ AIRCRAFT FACTORIES

✿ BALL BEARING PLANTS

⛽ OIL REFINERIES

⛴ U-BOAT YARDS

RUSSIA

Ploesti
Bucharest

BLACK SEA

BULGARIA

Ankara

;EAN
EA

TURKEY

CYPRUS

CRETE

Fayid

EGYPT

MAP BY ARGENZIANO ASSOCIATES

bombs hanging there. Guns and bombs in place, the Fortresses were now weapons of mass destruction.

The fliers waited nervously, clustering around the bombers, smoking and talking and trying not to think of what lay ahead. At last it was time to take their stations. As a flare shot upward from the control tower, each pilot and copilot began the complicated operation of bringing a twenty-seven-ton Flying Fortress alive.

Engine cooling flaps, fuel valves, carburetor controls, propeller settings —these and scores of other things were checked or adjusted. Then, each copilot pushed the button to start his number-one engine (the four engines were numbered from left to right and started in that order). As the electric starter turned the propeller, fuel was pumped into the engine; then the copilot flipped the switch to mesh propeller and engine—like putting a car into gear—and number one caught with a roar and a cloud of exhaust smoke. The operation was repeated for the other three motors. All around the edge of the field Fortresses coughed into life, a hundred or so engines

This map portrays Europe in mid-1942, when Hitler's empire was at its height and American daylight bombing experts began to select targets in Germany. Within eighteen months, Allied armies seized airfields at Benghazi in Libya and invaded Italy. By the end of 1943, the U.S. Fifteenth Air Force in Italy had joined the veteran Eighth Air Force in England in the assault on Germany.

15

These Flying Fortresses taxiing to the take-off line were photographed at an English air base in 1943. An hour was allotted for the bombers to start engines and then taxi into their proper positions, and also to allow for mishaps—on occasion a pilot ran one of his wheels off the edge of the runway and had to be towed out of the mud by a tractor.

blending into a ragged and deafening chorus.

Bottom turret gunners locked their guns facing rearward, clear for taxiing, the wheels were unblocked, and the B-17s began to trundle off their hardstands. It took a full hour to get the twenty-odd planes of a bomber group lined up for takeoff, which meant more nerve-racking waiting. Each pilot attached his plane in turn to the procession. Outboard engines

racing and brakes squealing, the Fortresses lumbered along nose-to-tail like circus elephants.

Finally, at 9:30 A.M., came the flare signaling takeoff. Thirty seconds apart, the B-17s roared down the runway and climbed into the morning sky. They tucked up their wheels and began to assemble in formation for the 350-mile flight to Bremen.

The air armada grew as the three other bomber groups assigned to Mis-

sion Number 52 slipped into position. Exactly on schedule, climbing steadily, 115 Flying Fortresses crossed the English coast and headed out over the North Sea. At 10,000 feet each crewman donned a rubber mask and plugged his air hose into the plane's central oxygen supply.

Just as a porcupine rolls itself into a ball to present a compact mass of sharp spines to its enemies, the bomber formation tightened up as it neared the danger zone. Smoke spurted briefly from the planes as gunners test-fired their machine guns, the single guns stuttering abruptly, the twin guns in the turrets pounding in steady rhythm. A smell like that of spent fireworks drifted through the ships.

The formation droned along four miles above the gray expanse of the North Sea. The airmen, grotesquely bundled in heavy boots, heated flying suits and gloves, helmets, and oxygen masks against the 30° below zero temperature, scanned their assigned sectors of sky for German fighters.

The first sign of the enemy was unexpected and unnerving. Ahead and off to one side a black-painted aircraft sauntered along, staying well out of range and obviously tracking the formation. It was a Flying Fortress repaired by the Germans after crash-landing in Europe on a previous mission. This ominous sentinel was radioing the course, speed, altitude, and size of the attacking force to the Luftwaffe defense network.

In war artist Peter Hurd's painting, two English farmers methodically go about their haying near an Eighth Air Force base while U.S. Flying Fortresses climb into the sky just above their heads.

As the Frisian Islands off the Dutch coast appeared on the horizon, the black rogue Fortress departed and was replaced by an unwelcome escort of German single-engine fighters that took over the spotting duties. The fighters skittered back and forth like insects on a pond, slowing their speed to match that of the bombers. Bremen was less than an hour's flying time away as the B-17s crossed the enemy-held coast.

Except for scattered and inaccurate flak, they remained free of attack. Time seemed to stand still. Then, almost over Bremen, the enemy struck and struck hard. The peaceful sky was suddenly filled with more than 150 snarling fighters. Flak flashed and smoked around the bomber formation like strings of Fourth-of-July firecrackers.

The Fortresses trembled as their gunners returned the fighters' fire.

Interphones crackled with sightings: "FWs twelve o'clock high! . . . Watch those two 109s at nine o'clock!" To coordinate defenses against attacking fighters, the men had been trained to imagine a giant clock laid atop the bomber, face up, with twelve o'clock dead ahead and six o'clock dead astern. Thus, "FWs twelve o'clock high" alerted gunners to Focke-Wulf 190s attacking the nose of the bomber from above, and "Two 109s at nine o'clock" meant Messerschmitt 109s coming in from the left side at the same level as the B-17.

The agile fighters swarmed around the attackers. Because of their great speed in relation to the bombers (at over 400 miles per hour they were traveling twice as fast as the B-17s), the fighters looked to the American fliers as if they were skidding through the air as they made firing passes.

Most attacks were launched from

Above: A Luftwaffe Focke-Wulf 190 fighter (right) races in for a frontal attack on a group of Flying Fortresses raiding Bremen. At the lower right is the wing of the Fortress from which the photograph was taken.

Below: As its bombs fall on Germany, a B-17 is bracketed by flak bursts. An American pilot said that antiaircraft shells exploding this close "sounded like somebody slamming a door at the end of a long hall."

head-on, successive flights of fighters charging in line-abreast formation with guns winking brightly as they fired their explosive cannon shells and machine gun bullets. Some came in on their backs and broke down and away after firing; others whipped straight on through the formation, twisting like corkscrews. Each of these individual attacks was over in a matter of seconds.

Gaps began to appear in the American formation. A B-17 with one wing burning fiercely glided downward and its crewmen tumbled out of the hatches, their parachutes opening as they fell. Other fliers were not so lucky; when fire or a cannon shell exploded a fuel tank, or when an out-of-control Fortress fell straight down in a tight spiral, no one got out alive. Here and there a shattered German fighter traced a great smoking arc as it plunged toward the ground.

The bombers plodded on, nearing the Focke-Wulf factory. Their bomb bay doors swung open. The German pilots redoubled their efforts, flying recklessly through their own flak to press home attacks. This was the moment of decision. The whole purpose of this armada of B-17s was distilled into just ninety seconds—the bombing run over the target.

In that critical minute and a half, the planes were flown on orders from

Floyd Davis' 1943 painting shows a burning, battered B-17 landing at its home field. The flares mean that wounded are aboard; an ambulance will meet the bomber the moment it lands. Other Fortresses await turns to land.

the bombardiers crouched over their bombsights, and the pilots had to fly them straight and level with no evasive maneuvers to avoid enemy fighters or flak. To tighten up the bomb pattern, all the bombardiers in a group "toggled on the leader"—that is, they released their own bombs the moment they saw the first bomb drop from the lead plane. If the leader was hit during the bombing run, the target would suffer fewer hits.

In spite of the vicious opposition of the fighters, the B-17s stayed in good formation. More than 260 tons of high-explosive bombs spewed out of their bomb bays. Below, the sprawling Focke-Wulf factory was blanketed by quick flashes and churning clouds of black smoke. Half-completed fighters on the assembly lines were ripped apart by the explosions or crushed by collapsing roofs and walls. Flames lighted the pall of smoke over the target.

The Flying Fortresses wheeled away from Bremen, the job they set out to do well done; now they had to battle their way home. German fighters still bored in, concentrating now on the looser formations and on the cripples limping along with one or two engines shot out.

For many bomber crewmen the return flight was agony. Fully half of the surviving B-17s were damaged. Pilots fought to keep battered hulks aloft, and flight engineers juggled valves to shift fuel from the tanks of shot-out engines to those still running,

This is a German picture of bomb damage in Bremen. The city made submarines and synthetic oil as well as warplanes, and was repeatedly bombed by the Allies. By 1945 it was more than 60 per cent destroyed.

set for full power and gas-hungry. Some planes carried dead and wounded men, lying in frozen pools of their own blood.

The German fighter attacks continued until the Fortresses picked up their escort of friendly fighters near the Dutch coast. The British Spitfire pilots approached the bombers cautiously, banking to show the distinctive shape of their wings. They had learned from bitter experience that Yank gunners shot at anything with one engine and asked questions later.

Over their home fields the bombers of each group circled for landing positions. The cripples came straight in; so did Fortresses with wounded aboard, signaling with red flares that they needed ambulances. Wheels and wing flaps down, the great ships slid out of the sky onto the runways and taxied to their hardstands. The fliers crawled through the hatches, their faces etched with exhaustion. As they climbed wearily into trucks for the ride to interrogation, ground crews swarmed over the bombers to begin the job of patching and repairing and replacing, of making each Flying For-

At bomber bases in England there were always "hangar queens" like this B-17 that had crash-landed. As Peter Hurd's painting shows, such wrecks were stripped of equipment needed to repair other Fortresses.

tress whole again for the next mission.

At interrogation the crews munched sandwiches and drank coffee while they waited their turn with the intelligence officers. As the forms were filled in Mission Number 52 became part of history: bombing altitude and release time, hits on the target, flak, formation position, fighter sightings, fighters claimed, losses.

The Fortress gunners claimed 62 German fighters shot down and listed another 15 as "probables." The Luftwaffe actually lost no more than a quarter of that total over Bremen on April 17. In the heat of combat, gunners were likely to claim nearly every fighter they took a shot at. When a fighter did go down, the gunners in all the nearby bombers concluded that it must have been their bullets that scored the kill.

Nine Fortresses turned back because of mechanical failures of one sort or another; 106 bombed Bremen. Sixteen of the Fortresses were shot down. One out of every seven American airmen who stumbled out of bed in the chill dawn to prepare for Mission Number 52 did not return.

Takeoff in a British bomber: the radioman is in the foreground, behind him is the navigator, and in the background are the pilots. The RAF was the senior partner in the Allied strategic air campaign, having dropped over 65,000 tons of bombs on Hitler's Europe by the time American bombers joined the attack.

2

THE ALLIES' BATTLE PLAN

Mission Number 52 summed up in a nutshell both the promise and the problems of the American air offensive against Hitler's Germany. The bombing had been highly effective. From photographs taken by reconnaissance planes and from reports by spies within Germany, Eighth Air Force intelligence officers learned that half the Focke-Wulf factory was demolished, cutting back fighter production at Bremen for months.

Set against this success were the losses—fifteen per cent of the attacking force. This was three times what air force leaders thought was an acceptable risk in daylight precision bombing. And a large part of America's war effort was tied to the success or failure of that controversial strategy.

Air striking forces are divided into two types, tactical and strategic. A tactical air force supports ground forces by attacking enemy troops and their battlefield lifelines—railroads, bridges, roads, and so on. Strategic bombing is aimed at the enemy's vitals—his cities, his war industries, his natural resources. Its goal is to make it impossible for a nation to support any of its armed forces.

In the opinion of some of America's leading military thinkers, strategic bombing had to be carried out in daylight to be really effective. They said that fleets of four-engine heavy bombers, operating in daylight with accurate bombsights at high altitudes, could efficiently knock to pieces Adolf Hitler's German war machine.

The U.S. Army Air Force had been nourishing this daylight bombing theory for a long time. Its roots went back to the years before the war. In the 1930s, when American military policy was based on the defense of the continental United States, a purely tactical air force satisfied old-line military men. But the AAF demanded a strategic bomber, and in 1935 got it—the Boeing B-17 Flying Fortress.

AAF leaders saw this plane as the answer to their dreams. If war broke out, they said, it might start in Europe or Asia, but eventually it would involve the United States. They wanted to be able to carry the fight to the enemy by means of strategic bombing, and they wanted to do so in daylight using the Flying Fortress.

At the time, however, there was little support for such thinking. Most Americans were satisfied to let the other countries of the world fight their own battles, and so the Army Air Force's budget included little money for strategic bombers. The AAF was able to buy only a handful of B-17s to test its ideas on daylight precision bombing.

Thus, in September, 1939, when Nazi Germany opened World War II, the AAF's situation was not very promising. Of all its combat planes on hand, just one type, the Flying Fortress, proved of any use in the coming air war over Europe. And there were exactly 23 B-17s in the American arsenal.

The United States was shocked by the Nazis' rapid, brutal victory march across Europe. Suddenly it seemed only a matter of time before America would have to fight. The nation began frantically to rearm; B-17s were snapped up by the armed forces as fast as Boeing Company workers could turn them out. Urgency changed attitudes, and as an air force historian has remarked, by 1940 the United States "had more money than time."

The Flying Fortresses that eventually went to war in 1942 were a considerable improvement over the experimental models of a few years before. Their top speed was raised from 256 to 317 miles per hour (normal

This cutaway view shows the crew positions in a Flying Fortress. From nose to tail are the bombardier, navigator, pilot and copilot, top turret gunner, radioman, ball turret gunner, the waist gunners, and the tail gunner. This is the B-17G, the Fortress model that entered combat in late 1943. It had a new twin-gun nose turret to meet the threat of frontal attacks often used by Luftwaffe fighters.

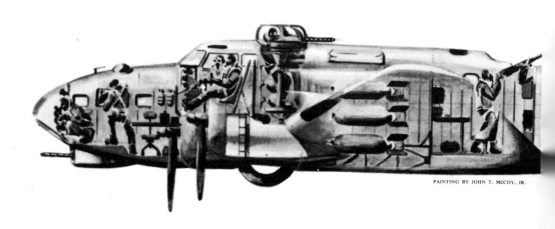

PAINTING BY JOHN T. McCOY, JR.

cruising speed was about 100 miles per hour less). Their bomb load was doubled, and their defensive armament upped from five light weapons to a dozen heavy .50 caliber machine guns.

A second American four-engine bomber was to play a role in the air war over Europe. This was the ungainly, slab-sided Consolidated B-24 Liberator, which was put into production in 1941. The Liberator carried a larger bomb load and had a greater range than the Flying Fortress; however, it was less heavily armed and armored, and it had a tendency to catch fire more easily when damaged in action.

Before the AAF had a chance to try out the Fortress and the Liberator, its pet theory of daylight bombing was put to the test of war by the air forces of both Germany and England.

In the late summer of 1940, shortly after Nazi forces sliced through all opposition to knock France out of the war, Reichsmarshal Hermann Goering sent his Luftwaffe bombers droning over the English Channel to cripple Britain and leave it open to invasion by the German army. Goering's bombers attacked in broad daylight, heavily escorted by fighters. Rising to meet them were the pilots of the Royal Air Force's Fighter Command. These indomitable fliers were the "few" in Prime Minister Winston Churchill's immortal tribute, "Never in the field of human conflict was so much owed by so many to so few."

The Battle of Britain, as this daylight air war came to be known, lasted two months. In savage and desperate encounters high over the green Eng-

A German artist sketched Dornier bombers over London in 1940. The Luftwaffe was winning the Battle of Britain by its attacks on RAF airfields and radar stations; then Goering switched to bombing cities.

lish countryside, RAF Hurricanes and Spitfires riddled the enemy formations. British losses were appalling; Luftwaffe losses—over 1,200 planes—were unbearable. Unable to gain mastery of the air, Hitler had to put aside his invasion plan.

Defeated in daylight, Goering turned to night attacks in an attempt to devastate London and other great cities, and to break the fighting spirit of the English people. But, like the RAF's pilots, the British civilians were tough. Tens of thousands of people were killed in the Blitz—short

for *blitzkrieg*, a German word meaning "lightning war." Great sections of London were knocked flat or burned out; cities like Coventry and Liverpool were devastated. Still, the English came up fighting. Winston Churchill, inspecting the ruins and making his "V for Victory" sign, spoke for his people.

The RAF's Bomber Command thoughtfully watched the failure of Goering's day bombing experiment. When its own daylight raids against the Continent met the same result, the RAF, too, limited its air assaults

In the Battle of Britain RAF Spitfires (above) fought off the German fighters as slower Hurricanes hit the bombers. Some Spitfires, like these, used cannon in the fighting, but most had eight machine guns.

to the nighttime hours. The British reasoned that their planes, which carried heavy bomb loads but were slow and lightly armed, could only operate safely under cover of darkness. The great industrial centers in Germany's Ruhr Valley were too big to miss even on the blackest nights. If the bombs fell wide of the factories, they still wrecked the nearby homes of workmen and paralyzed water, gas, and electrical services.

This tactic—called area bombing—was challenged on humanitarian grounds, especially after the RAF's first 1,000-plane raid, in May of 1942, laid waste the center of Cologne and killed or seriously injured over a thousand German civilians. Yet the horror of the Blitz was an ugly, bitter memory to the British people and their military leaders, and the spirit of revenge was strong. In any case, the RAF had little choice in the matter. Its equipment was suited only to nighttime attacks.

Britain's military planners, like their American counterparts, supported a strategic bombing offensive against Germany. It seemed the only way to

strike directly at the Nazi homeland for a long time to come. The British army, which had been so badly mauled in France, needed time to rebuild and to reinforce its beleaguered outposts throughout the world. America, catapulted into the war by the Japanese attack on Pearl Harbor on December 7, 1941, had to arm herself and transport her fighting forces across the Atlantic to England. In the meantime the heavy bombers would have to carry the fight to the enemy.

If the two allies agreed on the principle of a bombing offensive, they did not agree at all on how to carry it out. The RAF insisted that no heavy bombers, British or American, could fly deep into Germany in daylight and defend themselves against enemy fighters. Long-range escort fighters, the British felt, were absolutely necessary if daylight bombing was to have a chance of success. Neither country had such a fighter.

AAF leaders refused to be held

Douglas A-20 light bombers coming in low during military maneuvers in North Carolina a month before Pearl Harbor. At the left is a B-24 Liberator; and at far right are outmoded navy biplanes. The AAF had B-17s and B-24s in production at this time, but its modern fighters were still being developed.

11, 1942, thirteen heavily loaded Liberators lumbered off the runway of an airfield at Fayid, Egypt. One by one they headed northward across the Mediterranean Sea. Their target lay 1,300 miles away—the vast complex of oil refineries at Ploesti, Rumania. Not only was this the first American air strike at Nazi-held Europe, but it was the longest bombing raid so far undertaken in the war.

That June America had been at war six months. Thus far it had been a war of disasters and humiliations. After staggering the U.S. Navy's Pacific Fleet at Pearl Harbor the previous December, Japan had gone about gathering up Allied strongholds in the Pacific and the Far East like so many ripe plums. In the European theater of war the situation was no better. Most of Europe lay under Adolf Hitler's heel. Some 100 divisions of his army were readying a massive new offensive against Russia. In North Africa German General Erwin Rommel was threatening Egypt itself.

The Ploesti mission was a desperate act to meet a desperate situation. The B-24s had originally been sent out on a wildly optimistic scheme to avenge the Pearl Harbor defeat by bombing

back. They felt the only way to settle the issue was to put daylight bombing to the test once more—even without escort fighters. An RAF leader remarked that the Americans had "hung their hats on the day bomber policy and are convinced they can do it." Further argument, he warned, "would only cause irritation and make them very obstinate."

It fell to the B-24 Liberator to draw first blood in the American air assault on Hitler. Late on the night of June

Tokyo. The unit made its way from Florida to Africa. That was as close as it ever got to Tokyo, for Japanese troops captured the Chinese airfields the bombers were to use.

Casting about for another target to strike, the Allied high command settled on Ploesti. Its oil refineries produced one-third of the fuel for Hitler's army and air force. Even a partially successful attack would give a much-needed lift to the gloomy war situation.

Planning for the mission was hurried and haphazard. Neither the airmen nor their planes had been tested in combat. The flight plan was penciled in on a tattered National Geographic Society map of the Middle East. Nothing was said of Ploesti's defenses, for nothing was known of them.

After the takeoff from Fayid, the men in the Liberators had little time to worry about the odds against them. They were too busy staying on course and trying to keep warm. In one plane a gunner was discovered unconscious, his oxygen mask frozen; a fellow crewman found another mask just in time to save his life. A bombardier sacrificed his flight jacket to cover the bombsight so that its mechanism would not freeze. At dawn navigators checked their plotted courses against landmarks. They were over Rumania.

At this point the mission began to go sour. One B-24 suffered a mechanical failure and turned back. The other twelve pushed on toward Plo-

esti, only to run into heavy clouds near the target.

Each pilot met this problem in his own way. Some bombed blindly through the clouds, crossing their fingers and hoping that they might hit something. Others dove through the overcast to drop their bombs. Neither method scored many hits on the refineries.

Now the mission became a battle against time, a battle to reach friendly territory before fuel ran out. Nine Liberators managed to land safely in Allied-held Syria or Iraq. The remaining B-24s, short of gasoline, had to settle for neutral Turkey.

One of the big bombers caused a sensation by landing at the municipal airport in the Turkish capital city of Ankara. In a short time two more B-24s showed up, trailed by a German Messerschmitt fighter. The ME-109, which had been in hot pursuit all the way from Ploesti, followed the Liberators in for a landing. The fighter pilot stamped out of his cockpit in a rage. He too was out of gas.

Eventually the Turks recovered from their astonishment and interned the crews of all the planes. Internment was supposed to last for the duration of the war, but the Americans began escaping by twos and threes. The Turks finally gave up and shipped the remaining fliers back to Egypt.

The Ploesti mission was a brave but forlorn effort. Twelve of the thirteen Liberators reached the target—a

remarkable feat, considering the distance involved and the sketchy planning—and no crewmen were lost. Yet the oil refineries were almost unharmed. All the same, the first step had been taken and the first lessons learned. Fourteen months later the Americans would strike again at Ploesti.

The gallant exploit of the Ploesti raiders was quickly forgotten in the frenzied struggle to establish the Eighth Air Force in England. During the spring and summer of 1942, planes, bombs, ammunition, and spare parts were rushed across the Atlantic from the United States. Bases

The first U.S. air attack on Europe made the headlines two days after the raid. Despite military secrecy, reports from Turkey guessed that Ploesti was the target. But the bombers' home base remained a mystery.

were built and staffed, combat and ground crews trained, and a system of traffic control set up to regulate flights in the crowded air over England. Military intelligence units studied German industry and defenses, and pinpointed the best targets to bomb. Major General Carl Spaatz, commander of the Eighth, and Brigadier General Ira Eaker, head of its Bomber Command, worked furiously to put all the pieces of the puzzle together.

35

Above: Sir Arthur Harris (left), of RAF Bomber Command, seen with Eighth Air Force generals Spaatz (center) and Eaker.

Below: In October, 1942, when this B-17 assembly line was photographed, the need for bombers was far greater than the supply.

After weeks of exasperating delays, the Eighth Air Force was ready to go to war. Mission Number 1 was set for August 17, 1942. On that date, high-ranking officers of the American and British air forces gathered at Grafton Underwood air base near London. Colonel Frank Armstrong was to lead the mission, with General Eaker flying as observer in a B-17 nicknamed *Yankee Doodle.*

In mid-afternoon *Yankee Doodle* and eleven other Fortresses lifted off the airfield, climbed high over the English Channel, and headed for German-occupied France. Several squadrons of British Spitfires cruised overhead, shepherding them into enemy territory.

With little opposition from flak, the twelve Flying Fortresses went into their bombing run 23,000 feet above the railroad yards of Rouen, the medieval city where Joan of Arc had died in her fight to liberate France five centuries before. Bombardiers peered into their bombsights and released eighteen and a half tons of high explosives. Half the bombs exploded in fiery mushrooms right on target. Repair shops collapsed and machinery blew apart; strings of freight cars were smashed to splinters.

The escorting Spitfires rushed to the rescue as a handful of German fighters rose to give battle, and brief dogfights cartwheeled across the afternoon sky. A few interceptors made cautious passes at the unfamiliar American bombers. The gunners drove them off before they did any damage.

Back at Grafton Underwood the tension was high. Finally, at 7 P.M., as long shadows slanted across the runways, the drumming of engines could be heard. All twelve of the B-17s swept over the field and came in to land. Ground crews dashed out to the big planes and swarmed over the grinning fliers. Someone said it looked like a hometown crowd greeting the football team after a big victory.

Rouen was indeed a victory, although a small one. Outside of a few holes from flak, and two men slightly injured when a plexiglass nose canopy was shattered in a mid-air collision with a pigeon, planes and crews were undamaged. Considering that it was their first time in action, the bombing accuracy was excellent. Sir Arthur Harris, head of the RAF's Bomber Command, wrote General Eaker: "Yankee Doodle certainly went to town and can stick yet another well-deserved feather in his cap."

The Ploesti and Rouen raids signaled that the battle was joined. In time the daylight war between the U.S. Army Air Force and the German Luftwaffe would reach titanic proportions, and have a decisive effect on the outcome of World War II. The AAF, however, faced a long struggle before it could even become an equal partner with the RAF in the air assault on Hitler's Germany.

In the six weeks following the Rouen raid, the Eighth Air Force flew a dozen more short missions against

37

targets in occupied France. Results were promising: the bombing was generally accurate, the Luftwaffe opposition generally light. Only two bombers were lost.

The fourteenth and biggest attack took place on October 9, 1942, aimed at the steel mills and locomotive works at Lille in northern France. Over 100 B-17s and B-24s took off to hit the target. Swarms of German fighters tore through them, shot down four, and ruined the bombardiers' accuracy. Lille proved to be a high-water mark in the early history of the Eighth Air Force; six months were to pass before it could again attack in such strength.

In November, a month after the Lille mission, U.S. forces landed in North Africa in the hope of trapping Rommel's German army between the Americans advancing from the west and the British advancing from the east. The North African landing required tactical air support, and the Eighth Air Force had to provide most of it. "We were torn down and shipped away," General Eaker complained. Before Rommel was finally conquered, in May of 1943, the campaign had absorbed 27,000 seasoned airmen and mechanics from the Eighth, as well as many of its combat planes.

As a result, the American air offensive against Germany slumped badly at the end of 1942. Equally discouraging, the few heavy bombers available were being sent against a type

U.S. AIR FORCE

of target they could not hope to destroy.

During the winter of 1942–43, German submarine wolf packs roamed the Atlantic sea lanes, slaughtering merchant ships and tankers and threatening to strangle the vital flow of American arms to England and North Africa. The bombers were ordered to fight this menace by attacking submarine bases and construction yards.

Three combat formations of American heavy bombers soar high over the clouds on their way to strike Nazi Germany. Flying at an altitude of some four miles, they paint the sky with streaks of water vapor called contrails.

The U-boats were refueled, re-armed, and repaired in massive "sub pens," roofed over with as much as twelve feet of reinforced concrete, on the French coast. For months the Eighth Air Force beat its head against this unyielding concrete; the American fliers compared the whole thing to bouncing marbles off a sidewalk.

Raids on submarine construction yards were not too successful either, although at least they were made on the enemy's homeland. On January 27, 1943, American planes dropped their first bombs on Germany, attacking the shipyards at Wilhelmshaven. Colonel Frank Armstrong, the leader of Mission Number 1 at Rouen, piloted the first B-17 to cross the German border. One eager gunner marked the occasion by firing a few random shots, from 25,000 feet up, at Adolf Hitler's Third Reich.

The Wilhelmshaven raid was the first step in fulfilling a pledge. A few days before, a high-level conference had ended at Casablanca in North Africa, where President Franklin D. Roosevelt met with Prime Minister Churchill to hammer out new war strategy. During the conference General Eaker accomplished a feat not too often achieved during World War II—changing Winston Churchill's mind.

The bulldog-like Churchill was deeply depressed about American daylight bombing. They had been at it for half a year, he pointed out, and not a single bomb dropped on Germany itself. He urged the Americans to forget daylight bombing, and add their B-17s and B-24s to the British night bombing offensive. Eaker was called to the conference, saw the Prime Minister alone, and, as Churchill later wrote, "pleaded his cause with skill and tenacity."

Eaker reminded Churchill that the American bombers had been designed, and their crews trained, for daylight bombing. He ticked off other arguments: day bombing was the most precise way to demolish Germany's key war industries; important targets set afire by the AAF in daylight could easily be spotted and destroyed by the RAF after nightfall; dividing the bomber offensive relieved the congestion on airfields and in the limited air space over England. Finally, Eaker said, bombing around the clock would give the German defenses no rest.

"Bombing around the clock"—the eloquent Churchill liked the turn of phrase. Eaker's plea for time to test the theory of precision bombing and his pledge to begin hitting Germany itself won over the Prime Minister.

Gradually the pace began to quicken in the early months of 1943. Missions steadily increased in size and effectiveness. Yet serious problems remained. The weather caused constant trouble—English weather being a shattering experience for anyone who is not an Englishman—and not all the American planes reached the targets. Bombers also had to "abort," or turn back, for reasons ranging from engine trouble to frozen gun turrets. And German resistance grew more fierce.

Mission Number 52, against Bremen in April, proved that the AAF's daylight precision attacks could deliver knockout blows. But at Bremen the Luftwaffe proved that it too carried a lethal punch. The preliminaries were over; the main event was on.

40

Above: A German artist sketched the dedication of a synthetic oil refinery at Magdeburg in 1937. Because of Germany's shortage of petroleum, Hitler built many such plants to produce oil from coal. Magdeburg became a prime target for daylight raids.

Below: U.S. planes repeatedly bombed massive concrete "sub pens" such as these along the French coast. "No dog nor cat is left in these towns," a German wrote in 1943 of the raids on St. Nazaire and Lorient. "Nothing but the submarine shelters remain."

PETER HURD

Three B-17s roar low over cheering ground crews in Return from Rouen, *painted by Peter Hurd to celebrate the Eighth Air Force's first mission. At left are a C-47 transport and an RAF Spitfire.*

3

DEFENDING THE THIRD REICH

When Nazi Germany collapsed in 1945, the Allies captured most of the Luftwaffe's records and questioned many of its leaders. Out of this mass of historical material one point emerged clearly: for six years the men of the German Air Force fought with courage and ingenuity despite leadership that was often inept.

In the 1920s and 1930s Germany was the most air-minded nation in the world. Limited by the victorious Allies to building only civilian planes after the First World War, it still managed to train the hard core of an air force in airline operations and glider clubs, and by sending officers to other countries (particularly Russia) for flight training. As the other European powers drifted into disunity and indecision in the late twenties and early thirties, German air power revived. In 1933 Adolf Hitler and his Nazi party took command of the nation and promised the German people a Third Reich that would last a thousand years.

Hovering at the Fuehrer's elbow was one of the few genuine war heroes in the Nazi movement, Hermann Goering. Around his neck Goering wore proudly the Pour le Mérite, Germany's highest military decoration, awarded for his services in World War I. He had been a fighter pilot ace in that war, shooting down 22 Allied planes. Hitler named him head of the new German Luftwaffe.

Ruthless, energetic, sometimes brilliant and always vain, Goering was one of the most influential men around Hitler. He made sure that his Luftwaffe received a major share of the resources being poured into the rearming of Germany. To a world suddenly uneasy at the rise of Fascist military power, Goering had words of reassurance. "The engine drone of

Portly and smiling, Hermann Goering talks to one of his airmen just back from a raid on England early in the war. Goering played several roles in World War II: head of the Luftwaffe, planner of Germany's economy, Hitler's yes-man. "If the Fuehrer wants it, two and two make five," Goering said.

45

PAINTING BY JOHN T. MCCOY, JR.

The graceful, maneuverable Focke-Wulf 190 was a mainstay of Luftwaffe fighter squadrons after 1941. This painting reveals its main features. Top speed was about 410 miles per hour. The pilot could get short bursts of extra speed by injecting a mixture of water and methanol into the 1,700 horsepower, 14-cylinder radial engine. Under the cockpit are fuel tanks; they were protected, as was the pilot, by armor plate. Behind the fuel tanks are oxygen tanks (shown in yellow). The wide-track wheels retracted inward. The FW-190 was armed with two machine guns above the engine and four 20 millimeter cannon in the wings equipped to fire 620 shells. The brown containers held ammunition. The FW-190D, a faster model with an in-line engine, came into use in 1944.

German fighter and defense squadrons will not disturb the symphony of peace," he purred.

By the end of 1935 the Luftwaffe had achieved equality with the air forces of Great Britain and France. Then it began to pull ahead. Equally important, it learned the invaluable lessons of combat by actively supporting the Fascist cause during the Spanish Civil War. In September, 1939,

46

tight control of the air over the battlefields.

The German Stuka dive bomber terrified ground troops. Here was surely one of the worst-looking airplanes ever designed, yet its very ugliness was an asset. It plunged out of the sky like a huge hawk with talons extended "with a roar like the Day of Judgment," as one man described it. But whether the Stuka could operate as effectively when there were enemy fighters in the air to shoot at it was a question still to be answered.

The answer to that question, and to others about the offensive power of the German Air Force, came during the Battle of Britain in 1940. For the first time the Luftwaffe suffered defeat. The Stukas were picked off by the RAF before they could drop their bombs. The bigger German bombers were too lightly armed to defend themselves. The Messerschmitt 109 fighter, roughly equal in fighting power to the British Spitfire and Hurricane, was badly hampered by its short range; Luftwaffe pilots repeatedly broke off combat to return to France before they ran out of gas.

Also in 1940, Hitler and Goering made a decision that eventually put the Luftwaffe in serious difficulty. Expecting only a short war, the Nazi leaders refused to put research and development of new weapons on a crash-program basis. Work was to be postponed on planes that could not be put into production within two years; "such types will not be

when Germany marched into Poland, the Luftwaffe was the most powerful air force in the world.

During the first year of the war the Third Reich was everywhere triumphant: Poland, Denmark, Norway, Holland, Belgium, and even once-mighty France fell before Hitler. Everywhere the Luftwaffe led the victory parade, its bombers and fighters crippling enemy air forces and keeping

47

wanted after the war," announced the Reich Air Ministry.

In 1942, however, when the American bomber offensive against Germany began, the Luftwaffe was still a very potent force. Most defense squadrons were equipped with either of two fighter types, the Messerschmitt 109 or the Focke-Wulf 190.

The ME-109 was the veteran of the German Air Force, having undergone its first military tests in October, 1935. (That same month the Flying Fortress was being tested by the U.S. Army at Wright Field in Ohio.) The angular, shark-like ME-109 was a formidable airplane. Perhaps its greatest advantage was a sound basic design that could take increasingly bigger, more powerful engines and heavier armament. The ME-109G, christened the Gustav by German pilots, was the version in production after 1942. At the altitudes flown by the American bombers it had a top speed of well over 400 miles per hour.

The Focke-Wulf 190 got in under the wire of Hitler's limitation on new designs. It was fortunate for the German Air Force that it did. The FW-190 went into production in 1941 and immediately proved superior to the Luftwaffe's arch enemy, the Spitfire. Almost as fast as the Gustav and more maneuverable, the beautifully proportioned FW-190 was a pilot's dream to fly and a mechanic's dream to service. Goering told designer Kurt Tank to "turn these new fighters out like so many hot rolls!"

Yet all the advantages of good fighter plane design—speed, maneuverability, rapid climbing ability, ruggedness—were wasted without adequate firepower. The Germans made careful studies of air armament. Their fighters (and Allied planes as well) were equipped with cameras that automatically operated whenever the guns were fired. By carefully examining these films German gunnery experts were able to develop the best combination of tactics and weapons.

One of the first things the experts discovered was that Allied bombers could absorb a great number of machine gun bullets and still keep flying. Something more potent was needed. They turned to rapid-firing air cannon using explosive shells. Luftwaffe fighters rolling off the assembly lines by 1943 were equipped with as many as four heavy cannon and two machine guns. The FW-190, especially, became a flying arsenal, with two or three times the firepower of the bombers it faced.

In the early months of 1943 the Germans grew increasingly concerned about Allied strategic bombing. The RAF's night raids were causing immense destruction throughout Germany. Night after night British bombers by the hundreds streamed over the Third Reich, leaving behind ruined factories and burning cities.

To combat the RAF the Luftwaffe needed more flak guns and more searchlights. Better radio and radar

A Stuka being serviced (above) on the Russian front was sketched by a German war artist. This "tank-busting" version of the famous Luftwaffe dive bomber has powerful antitank guns under its wings. The Messerschmitt 109 below is undergoing wind tunnel testing. Some 33,000 ME-109s were built, more than any other warplane.

A German painting records an almost nightly scene over the Third Reich. As searchlights probe the sky and flak crews man their guns, RAF "pathfinders" drop marking flares for bombers soon to come.

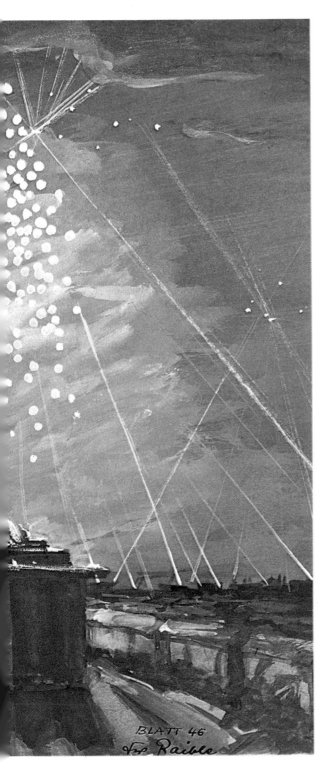

BLATT 46
für Raible

devices were required to locate the British bomber formations. Additional radar-equipped night fighters that could "see" in the darkness had to be built, and more airmen trained to use them.

If, at the same time, American daylight raids continued to grow in strength, the result would be a nightmare for Germany. Antiaircraft batteries would have to be manned around the clock, the number of fighter pilots doubled, and the civil defense units, to say nothing of the factory workers, would get no rest. The Luftwaffe had to make a desperate attempt to stop the Americans, to make their attacks so expensive that they could not be continued.

Hermann Goering set out to prove the wisdom of his remark that the Americans might be good at making Fords and Chevrolets and razor blades, but designing and building planes that could defeat the German Air Force was another matter. Goering began to mass his squadrons in Western Europe, equipping them with the latest-model fighters. Immense resources of manpower and war materiel were poured into new and more deadly antiaircraft batteries, radar equipment to warn of approaching raiders, and a complex fighter-control radio network to guide the interceptors to the American bombers.

At this point in the war, however, Nazi Germany was scraping near the bottom of the barrel. Planes and pilots transferred to the Third Reich

51

left German armies on the fighting fronts stripped of air cover. In Russia and North Africa Hitler's armies were halted or driven back. And Goering's orders to increase the production of fighter planes meant that raw materials had to be diverted from factories making rifles and trucks and tanks for the ground forces.

At first the Germans were puzzled about what tactics to use against the heavily armed American B-17s and B-24s. The fighter pilots began to experiment and very soon located a crack in the bombers' defense. They found that relatively few guns could be brought to bear against a frontal assault. When the fighters attacked the bombers head-on, the results could be deadly for the intruders.

A Luftwaffe fighter pilot named Heinz Knoke described the head-on tactics he used during an American raid on Wilhelmshaven in February, 1943. "The Yank is focused in my sights," Knoke wrote in his diary. "He grows rapidly larger. I reach for the firing buttons on the stick. Tracers come whizzing past my head. They have opened fire at me . . . . I press both buttons, but my aim is poor. I can see only a few hits register in the right wing. I almost scrape the fat belly as I dive past."

Knoke whipped his ME-109 around, raced ahead of the bomber formation again, and bored in for a second frontal attack on the Liberator he had picked for his victim. This time his aim was better. He broke away to watch the results of his second attack: "Flames are spreading along the bottom of my

Liberator. It sheers away from the formation in a wide sweep to the right. Twice more I come in to attack, this time from above the tail. . . . I watch my cannon shellbursts rake along the top of the fuselage and right wing. The inside engine stops. Suddenly the wing breaks off altogether. The body of the stricken monster plunges vertically, spinning into the depths."

Because of the short range of the German interceptors they had to be guided to the bombers with precision; otherwise, they would waste precious fuel hunting their quarry and have too little left to press an attack and return to base. German radar stations on the French and Dutch coasts picked up the American bombers as they approached the Continent. At

These pictures are from films taken by the automatic cameras of German interceptors. The sequence above shows a frontal attack on an American B-24. The fighter pilot's aim was deadly; the white spots mark his shells striking the B-24's nose and cockpit, and raking across the top of the fuselage as he sweeps over the bomber. Below is a rear attack on a Flying Fortress. The Luftwaffe pilot closed to point-blank range, hitting the B-17's left wing, setting the engines on fire, and knocking pieces from the tail.

OVERLEAF: *In Floyd Davis' painting, a majestic formation of Flying Fortresses nears Hamburg on July 25, 1943. A pillar of smoke (right) marks the target, still burning from an immense RAF fire raid the night before. The British had dispatched nearly 800 planes in a long, narrow column, so that bombs fell steadily for forty-five minutes. While civil defense units waited out the bombing, scores of fires raged unchecked and out of control.*

times spotter planes, like the captured Flying Fortresses used in the Bremen battle in April, provided valuable information. German fighter-control headquarters had divided occupied Europe into sections, and as the bombers were tracked inland, headquarters would order one squadron after another to take off and intercept in certain sectors.

At the airfields the pilots were alerted when the bombers first appeared on the screens of the coastal radar stations. Their fighters were lined up at the edge of the field, armed and fueled. When the takeoff signal was given, pilots sprinted to their planes, mechanics cranked the engines into life, and the fighters roared down the field half a dozen or more abreast.

The interceptors streaked upward toward their assigned altitude and sector. If all went well and the bombers had not changed course, the Germans arrived with plenty of fuel to find the great formations spread out before them. By skillful timing, Luftwaffe fighter-control could keep the U.S. bombers under constant attack to and from the target, replacing each group of fighters running low on gasoline with a fresh one. It was not uncommon for a squadron to hit the bombers on the way in, return to its field for more fuel and ammunition, and then catch the bombers again on their return flight.

Both sides constantly experimented with fighting tactics. At American bases in England mechanics put together various combinations of machine guns to meet the threat of frontal attacks. Back in the United States a nose turret mounting twin guns was rushed into production. Bigger and tighter formations were tried to increase defensive firepower.

The Germans, in turn, began to make frontal attacks on a wide front and in rapid succession to overwhelm the defenses. They also coordinated

56

their attacks to hit from several different directions at once. Often the Luftwaffe concentrated only on the less protected top and bottom groups in the combat formations.

The Germans also tried out new weapons. Twin-engine Messerschmitt 110s and Junkers 88s cruised along just outside the range of the bombers' guns, lobbing explosive rockets into the formations. Even the single-

What the crews of the B-17s in the painting on pages 54–55 saw when they reached Hamburg is pictured here. They tried to bomb submarine building yards along the Elbe River (lower right) through the smoke from the fire storm started by the RAF. A German fighter is circled at upper right.

"Where is Mrs. Brylla?" is the stark question chalked on a bombed-out house by a rescue worker seeking information about one of the thousands missing in Hamburg's ruins.

engine Messerschmitts and Focke-Wulfs fired rockets as a prelude to their close-in assaults. But perhaps the most novel idea was bombing the bombers.

This tactic began to appear early in 1943. Bombs were slung under the fuselages of the fighters, and the pilots aimed and dropped them at a certain height above the attacking formation. Time fuzes exploded the bombs when they had fallen to the altitude of the bombers. At first, American airmen regarded this bombing as more of a nuisance than a danger, but gradually the German pilots improved their aim, and the tactic became a serious threat.

Lieutenant Knoke recorded in his diary such an attack on a bomber force that had penetrated deep into Germany in July, 1943. "We climb over the approaching bombers and release our bombs," he wrote. "A fantastic scene is produced by the explosions. The close-flying formation is disorganized completely. Some of the Fortresses plunge down in steep dives, while others swerve off to the sides. They narrowly escape mid-air collision. The bomb dropped by Sergeant Fest explodes exactly in the center of a close flight of three heavy bombers. All three simultaneously go down to crash . . . .Our earphones resound with whoops of triumph . . . . We loop and roll above the enemy formation in sheer joy."

Despite increasing losses, by midsummer of 1943 the Allied bomber offensive was in high gear. The RAF's Bomber Command was thinking in terms of obliterating whole cities. The Eighth Air Force, its strength greatly increased since the spring, sent out hundreds of bombers every day the weather was clear. If the Nazi leaders needed an object lesson about the threat of around-the-clock bombing, they received it at Hamburg.

The ordeal of Germany's second largest city was one of the most ter-

58

rible in the history of the European air war. Between July 24 and August 3 the RAF launched four great night raids on the city; twice during that period the Eighth Air Force blasted it by day. An estimated 43,000 people were killed in the stricken city. The Battle of Hamburg became known throughout Germany as simply "*Die Katastrophe*."

The RAF sprang a major surprise on the defenders by scattering millions of strips of tinfoil to blind the German radar. Without radar guidance, the night fighters were nearly helpless; of some 3,100 British bombers sent to Hamburg on those four nights, only 86 were shot down. The Americans lost 27 B-17s.

In the grim balance sheet of war these losses were minor when set against what happened to the citizens of Hamburg. What they went through can be glimpsed in the experience of a German woman who was visiting the city and whose story was set down by her daughter.

The woman was driven from an underground bomb shelter by the direct hit of an incendiary bomb, and she and a mother with two small children were taken in hand by an old man.

"There were walls of flame around them now," the account reads. "One of the terrified children rushed down a side street. The mother followed, leaving her boy behind . . . the whole top floor of the house opposite crashed down on the two of them. The old man grabbed the boy's hand firmly.

'You come with us,' he ordered."

The three of them fled through the inferno to an open field, where they fell exhausted. Before long, however, the woman realized that the fire was catching up:

"A great flame was shooting straight out towards them. A flame as high as the houses and nearly as wide as the whole street. As she stared in fascination, the giant flame jerked back and then shot forward towards them again.

"'My God, what is it?' she said.

"'It's a fire storm,' the old man answered. 'Quick, come along, there's no time to lose. In a minute there will be dozens of flames like that and they'll reach us.'"

But it was too late for the little boy; he had suffocated as the fire storm greedily consumed the oxygen in the air. The woman and the old man finally managed to reach the safety of a nearby stream. The next morning they returned to the smouldering city.

There they saw rescue workers removing bodies from the wreckage and stacking them like cordwood in trucks. A woman standing near them shivered. "If there were a God," she said, "He would have shown some mercy to them." The old man replied sharply: "Leave God out of this. Men make war, not God."

This war that men made went on for almost two more years. Before it was finished, the bombers had visited virtually every city in Germany, and the defenders had fought them bitterly every step of the way.

4

TARGET: PLOESTI

The great oil refineries at Ploesti were never far from the thoughts of the men who planned the American bombing campaign. Producing a third of the Germans' fuel, the Rumanian city seemed to the American planners the perfect place to throw a monkey wrench into Hitler's war machine.

Ploesti had been the target of the first U.S. strategic raid on Europe in June of 1942. Although the dozen B-24s did little harm to the refineries, they at least had the range to reach them. This lesson was not lost on the Germans. They set out to turn Ploesti into the most heavily defended city in all of Europe.

By August 1, 1943 (as many fires still smoldered within the city of Hamburg), the stage was set for one of the classic battles of the Second World War. A powerful, well-trained American striking force, equipped with a daring plan of attack, was poised on the southern shore of the Mediterranean Sea. Almost 1,200 miles away, the skillful, well-trained defenders of Ploesti were in a high state of readiness.

Planning for the Ploesti raid—code-named Operation Tidal Wave—began early in 1943. It would have to be launched from somewhere in the Mediterranean area, for the refineries were beyond the reach of bombers flying from England. When the Germans were finally thrown out of North Africa that spring, air bases became available at Benghazi, in the part of Libya bulging out into the Mediterranean almost due south of Ploesti. Half the route from Benghazi lay over water, the other half over lightly defended Albania, Yugoslavia, and Bulgaria. Getting to the target, it was thought, should not be difficult.

Still, the distance posed a problem. Over nine tons of gasoline were needed by each Liberator to deliver two tons of bombs to Ploesti and return. Since fewer than 200 B-24s were available, it was unlikely that the usual high-altitude approach could place enough of the limited bomb load on the refineries to wipe them out. Finally, 1,150 miles was a long way to fly without detection; swarms of fighters

A B-24 Liberator of the Pyramiders bomber group skims a few feet above the chimneys of a blazing oil refinery at Ploesti. This particular refinery, one of many surrounding the city, was the largest in Europe. Half of it was wrecked by the American attackers.

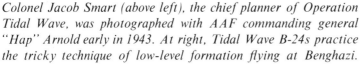

Colonel Jacob Smart (above left), the chief planner of Operation Tidal Wave, was photographed with AAF commanding general "Hap" Arnold early in 1943. At right, Tidal Wave B-24s practice the tricky technique of low-level formation flying at Benghazi.

would surely be waiting at the target.

Thus the problem. Tidal Wave's chief planner, Colonel Jacob Smart, came up with an ingenious solution— the B-24s would attack Ploesti at treetop level. At this height individual refineries, even the key installations within them, could be hit with the utmost precision; every bomb would count. The bombers could elude the German warning radar (at ground level radar was useless, for it picked up all kinds of traffic, including trucks and trains). Enemy flak gunners would be caught by surprise and subjected to the fire of the Liberators' gunners. Enemy fighters would be able to attack only from above.

Operation Tidal Wave, then, was to be flown at ground level, and the five

bomber groups assigned to the mission began to practice the technique. A pair of battle-tested Eighth Air Force Liberator outfits, known as the Eight Balls and the Traveling Circus, roared back and forth over the English countryside, terrifying cows and infuriating farmers.

In late June and early July the Tidal Wave force assembled at Benghazi. From England came the Traveling Circus and the Eight Balls, plus a group calling itself the Sky Scorpions, fresh from American training schools. They were greeted by two veteran Liberator groups of the U.S. Ninth Air Force, the Liberandos and the Pyramiders, who had cut their combat teeth fighting Rommel in the desert.

The Liberator men were put on a

rugged training schedule. They attended lectures, studied pictures and drawings, and went over and over their tactics. A huge mock-up of the Ploesti refineries was built in the desert and repeated practice attacks were made on it. On one occasion the fliers surprised a group of high-ranking officers in the target area and watched with malicious glee as the brass scrambled for cover while the B-24s howled over them.

As the Liberator crews perfected their low-level tactics at Benghazi, the Germans at Ploesti were equally busy. In command was a master of air defense named Alfred Gerstenberg. A World War I squadronmate and close friend of Hermann Goering, General Gerstenberg was able to obtain vir-

tually everything he asked for. According to a fellow officer, Gerstenberg had a one-track mind: "He worked sixteen hours a day with one goal in mind—to make Ploesti too costly for the enemy to attack."

The German general made two important decisions in planning his defenses. First, he saw that the threat from the east was slight, for Russia had no strategic air force. Secondly, he began to collect as many Luftwaffe airmen and flak gunners as he could lay his hands on. Although Rumania had joined the Axis powers, it was a reluctant partner and its soldiers were not noted for their eagerness to die for the German Fuehrer. Gerstenberg built Ploesti's strongest defenses south and west of the city, the direc-

63

The Liberators above get a final check at Benghazi. The navigator of Brewery Wagon, *the B-24 at left, found himself unexpectedly leading the Ploesti raid;* Brewery Wagon's *fate is recorded in the picture on page 73. The airmen below prepare for the takeoff.*

tions from which he expected any attacks to come, and he manned them with crack German troops. The Americans knew neither of these facts.

The sprawling oil refineries completely surrounded the city; ringing them in turn were Gerstenberg's defenses. His antiaircraft batteries mounted 237 guns, and hundreds of machine guns were concealed everywhere, from church steeples to haystacks. A so-called "flak train," bristling with guns, roamed the railroad lines around the refineries. Floating overhead were sausage-shaped barrage balloons trailing wires tied to charges that would explode if a plane brushed them. The fighter defenses included more than 50 late-model ME-109s, most of them flown by veteran German pilots. In the refineries themselves were concrete "blast walls" around all the key installations, and a first-class brigade of fire fighters.

A deciphered enemy radio message set the date for the Ploesti raid. In July the Allies managed to break the weather code used by the Luftwaffe. But since the code was changed every month, August 1 was the last date on which they could count on learning the weather over Ploesti.

Colonel Smart and the other men who planned the raid knew that they were taking a huge gamble in throwing this one-punch haymaker; everything, including luck, would have to work perfectly if it were to knock out Ploesti. The details were planned down to the last comma. What was missing was any real knowledge of the refineries' defenses. Still, their biggest secret—that the bombers would come in at ground level—was intact.

At dawn on Sunday, August 1, 1943, 178 heavily loaded Liberators rushed down the runways of the Benghazi airfields and took off at two-minute intervals. One B-24 suffered engine failure on takeoff and piled into a concrete pole. The others assembled in formation for the long flight over the Mediterranean.

Within an hour the high command at Ploesti knew that a big force of American bombers was airborne and heading north. The Germans had done some code cracking of their own; they picked up and deciphered a routine message sent out to warn Allied defenses in the area not to fire by mistake at the bomber force. Pilots and gunners at Ploesti were alerted to stand by for possible action.

Ten B-24s aborted with mechanical failures during the three-hour flight over the Mediterranean. Then, just before the armada reached the Albanian coast, there was a more serious mishap. The lead ship carrying the mission's navigator suddenly pitched violently, flipped over on its back, and plunged straight into the sea. The plane with the deputy navigator aboard dove down in a futile search for survivors, could not climb back fast enough to catch up with the formation, and had to turn back. A young officer in a B-24 named *Brewery Wagon* became mission navigator.

"Killer" Kane's Pyramiders race in to attack Ploesti, flying as low as possible to try and get under the deadly curtain of German ground fire. In the background a downed B-24 leaves a trail of burning gas.

Over Yugoslavia the bombers ran into a towering cloud bank. The two leading groups climbed to go over the top of the clouds; the other three elected to hedgehop close to the mountain peaks at lower altitudes. The high groups picked up a stiff tail wind and pulled farther and farther ahead. By the time the B-24s dipped down out of the mountains and streamed over the flatlands of the Danube River Valley, the Tidal Wave force had been hopelessly divided.

The bombers had been spotted and tracked, and the Germans, certain now that Ploesti was the target, prepared for action. Fighters began to take off to meet the enemy. As the Messerschmitts circled high over the predicted course of the bombers, the Liberators were racing over the tree-tops toward Ploesti.

In order to aid navigation, a series of three checkpoints had been selected and the crewmen briefed to spot them. At the third checkpoint, four of the five groups were to make a right turn and follow a railroad line leading straight into Ploesti. The fifth group, the Sky Scorpions, was to bear left and hit an isolated refinery a few miles to the north. What the planners had not bargained for, however, was that the three checkpoints, all small towns, looked a great deal alike. In addition, a ground haze made identification all the more difficult.

Only minutes from the target there occurred the day's most tragic error. The leading group, the Liberandos, took a wrong turn. Instead of going right at the third checkpoint, it turned at the second, twenty miles too soon. Hard on its heels came the Traveling Circus.

The only B-24 of these two groups that stayed on the right course was that of the young lieutenant who had inherited the navigating duties. But, apparently doubting the lieutenant's ability, the group leader had assumed control of the formation. The turn took the Liberators not toward Ploesti but toward the Rumanian capital of Bucharest, thirty-five miles away. It also led them straight into Gerstenberg's heaviest concentration of flak.

This wrong turn had two disastrous effects. The low-level approach was revealed too soon and the Ploesti defenders had time—just barely —to adjust to it. The second effect was to cause chaos over the target. Both the Liberandos and the Traveling Circus realized their mistake and wheeled around. But then they were approaching Ploesti from the wrong direction. Their new course was taking them head-on into the B-24 groups that had fallen behind over the mountains.

It was one of the Traveling Circus leaders, Lieutenant Colonel Addison Baker, who first realized the error and led his group into a screaming turn. By this time the Battle of Ploesti had begun. Flak gunners worked frantically to change the fuzes on their shells so that they would explode almost the moment they left the gun barrels. B-24 gunners saw fire spurting at them from everywhere—towers, haystacks, houses—and opened a deadly duel with the ground gunners.

Bombers staggered under the impact of exploding shells even as their machine guns sprayed bullets into the flak crews. One B-24, blazing like a Roman candle, crashed on top of a battery. Colonel Baker's Liberator, *Hell's Wench*, clipped a balloon cable, took hits from five antiaircraft shells, and burst into flames. Baker plunged on, leading the Traveling Circus to the target. Over the refineries, its mission finished, *Hell's Wench* stalled and piled up in a field. The entire crew was killed.

The Traveling Circus' Liberators dumped their bombs into the ring of refineries and then swept over Ploesti itself. Several crippled bombers careened down the city's streets, shedding their wings; one of them buried itself in the Ploesti women's prison, trapping scores of inmates in the ruins.

An American airman was amazed at the volume of ground fire. "I didn't see how anyone could get through that mess alive," he said later. In the flak batteries below, reported a German corporal ". . . it was bedlam. Our men were cheering and screaming." The bombers were so near the ground that a German gunner was able to open the breech of his heavy 88-millimeter weapon, sight through the barrel, slam in a shell, and knock down a B-24 with one shot.

A B-24 named *Utah Man* limped

Four Liberators can be seen above framed in smoke as they begin their bombing run. The refinery had been set afire by Traveling Circus airmen who missed their intended targets and hit this one instead; the explosions of their delayed-action bombs smashed several late-arriving B-24s. After the raiders had gone, German fire-fighters (right) went to work.

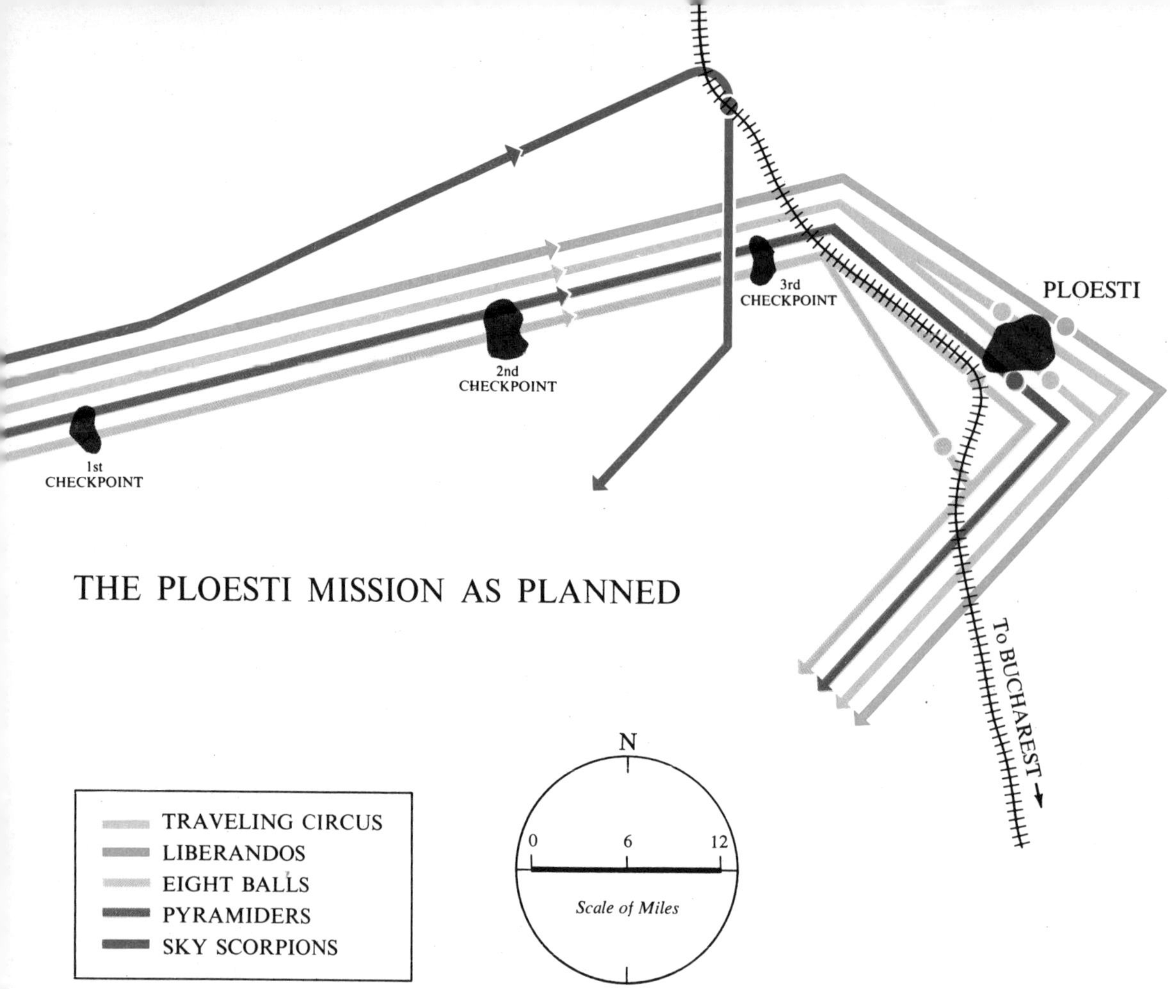

1st
CHECKPOINT

2nd
CHECKPOINT

3rd
CHECKPOINT

PLOESTI

To BUCHAREST

THE PLOESTI MISSION AS PLANNED

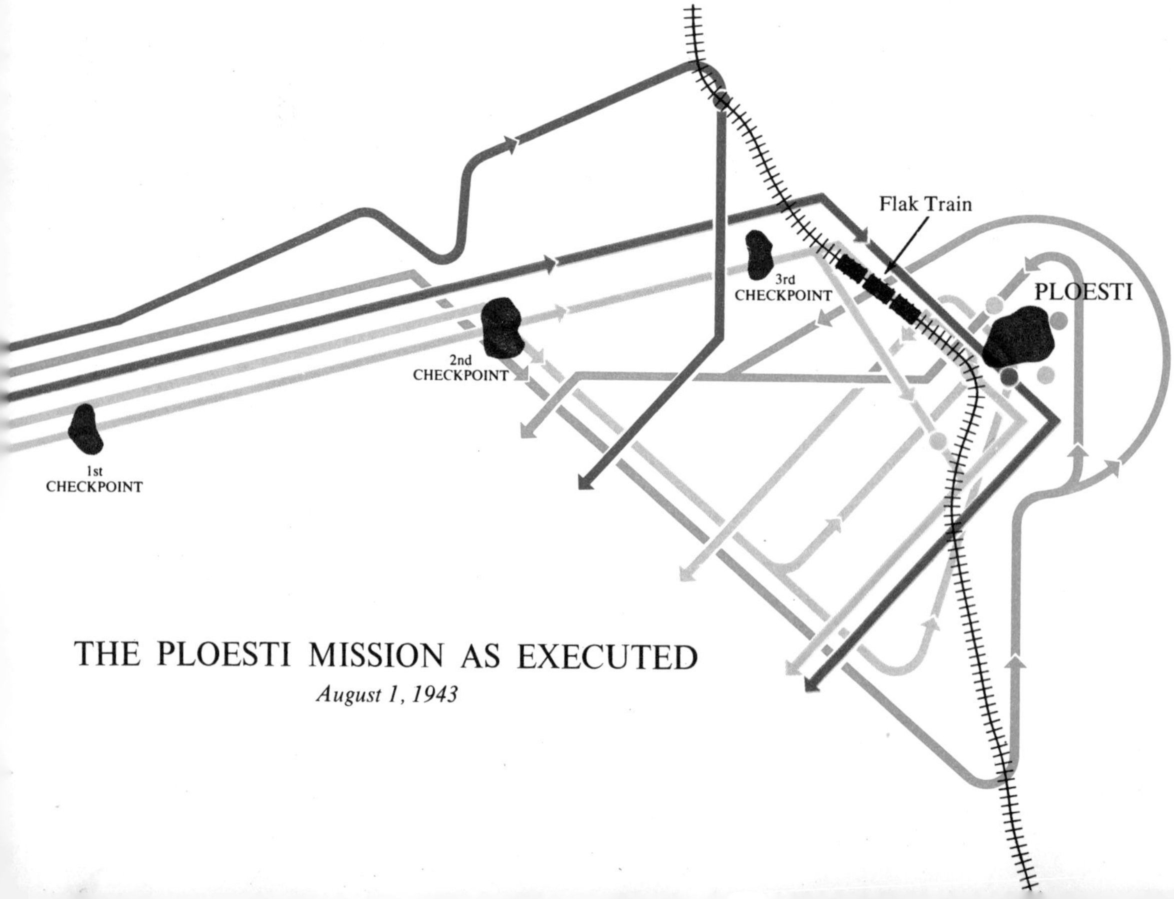

N

0   6   12

Scale of Miles

TRAVELING CIRCUS
LIBERANDOS
EIGHT BALLS
PYRAMIDERS
SKY SCORPIONS

Flak Train

3rd
CHECKPOINT

PLOESTI

2nd
CHECKPOINT

1st
CHECKPOINT

THE PLOESTI MISSION AS EXECUTED
August 1, 1943

CHART BY ARGENZIANO ASSOCIATES

away from the target with its fuselage riddled and gasoline streaming from a punctured wing tank. In its bomb bay were two live 1,000-pound bombs, triggered but stuck there because of a damaged release mechanism. The thousand-pounders were fuzed to go off in fifty minutes. (Like all the Ploesti raiders, *Utah Man*'s bombs had delayed-action fuzes so that they would not wreck following planes when they exploded.) Two crewmen crawled into the bomb bay and desperately hammered at the bombs until they finally knocked them loose. *Utah Man* was one of 15 Circus planes to survive the bombing run; 34 had begun it.

The Liberandos had almost reached Bucharest before they realized their error and turned around. As they approached Ploesti they witnessed the ordeal of the Traveling Circus ahead.

A Liberando pilot remembered seeing "flights of three or four, or single planes going in different directions, streaking smoke and flames, striking the ground, wings, tails, and fuselages breaking up, big balls of smoke rolling out of the wrecks before they stopped skidding." The Liber-

andos' commander radioed his pilots to forget their briefed targets—approaching from the wrong direction, they could not recognize them anyway—and to attack anything they could see.

At this point complete chaos descended on Ploesti. The high-flying Messerschmitts, aware at last of the bombers far below, screamed down to the attack. Some of the time-fuzed bombs began exploding. Oil tanks set afire by the planes' gunners spewed flames and billows of black smoke. As the Liberandos scattered to find targets and the Circus planes tried to get away, two more bomber groups, the Eight Balls and the Pyramiders, roared in from the opposite direction.

In seconds three separate layers of Liberators crisscrossed over Ploesti's rooftops, desperately dodging each other. Below, General Gerstenberg watched admiringly; he had no idea the Americans had not planned it all that way.

Both the Eight Balls and the Pyramiders, who had lagged behind over the mountains, had turned at the correct checkpoint and flown along the railroad track leading to Ploesti. Then they had a nasty surprise. Gerstenberg's flak train was chugging down the track as fast as it could go, spraying gunfire right and left at the passing bombers. B-24 gunners finally blew up the train's engine, but not before several planes had been mortally wounded.

A 16-plane element of the Eight

Balls somehow managed to find its assigned refinery and plant its bombs squarely on it. Since Traveling Circus planes had already hit the same target by mistake, the damage they did was devastating. Nine of the 16 Eight Balls were shot down. The other half of the group had even greater success in its bombing. "We were too low to miss," said one man. "We were five feet above the target." All the while dozens of German fighters were blazing away at the bombers.

The Pyramiders, the fourth bomber group scheduled to hit the Ploesti refineries, were led by a tough Texan named John Riley Kane. As "Killer" Kane spotted his target, "everything but the kitchen sink began to rise from the ground at us." Into the flames and smoke went the Pyramiders. A barrage balloon contact charge blew the wing off a Liberator. One of the B-24s flew low enough to clip off the guy wires of a smoke stack; another was not so lucky, failed to pull up in time, and crashed into an oil storage tank. Kane's Pyramiders destroyed half their target, but lost 22 planes doing it.

The Sky Scorpions, Tidal Wave's rookie bomber group from the United States, very nearly made a wrong turn of its own, but it corrected quickly and headed toward its target eighteen miles north of Ploesti. Its 29 planes ran the same fierce gantlet of ground fire as did the other groups, but at least it did not have to dodge other bombers or avoid burning oil tanks.

Its strike was perfectly executed, and destroyed the refinery completely—at a cost of six B-24s. One crew whose bomb bay doors were jammed shut simply dropped its bombs through them; the dangling wreckage of the doors snagged cornstalks as the Liberator scurried away.

It had taken twenty-seven minutes to bomb Ploesti. Now the surviving Liberators, some in formation, some alone, began the long flight back to Benghazi. Gerstenberg's fighters returned to their fields, their fuel exhausted. In the blazing refineries the fire fighters got to work, and nerveless specialists scurried from one unexploded bomb to another, gambling they could de-fuze them before they went off. The Battle of Ploesti was over, but the ordeal of the men of Tidal Wave had only begun.

Most bombers set out to return the way they had come, staying at nearly zero altitude over the Danube plain. One dipped a bit too low and plowed through a haystack; the pilot prudently raised his altitude to thirty feet. In the lull the fliers began to examine the damage and their chances of getting home. Half the planes were badly hit, and most of them carried dead or wounded men.

The grim mathematics of time versus gasoline convinced many cripples to seek Allied-held islands in the Mediterranean. "We landed at Cyprus on an uphill runway, feeling very good," reported the pilot of *Vagabond King*. "I turned off to find a place to

Arabs and their desert transportation (above) stare at a B-24 in North Africa. Brewery Wagon, *at the left, was one of 53 Liberators that never got back to Benghazi. A flak shell killed the young navigator who kept* Brewery Wagon *on course when the planes behind him made their wrong turn; a German fighter finished off the crippled bomber. Eight of the crewmen survived the crash and were taken to a Rumanian prisoner-of-war camp.*

park and a truck hit us. We were on a highway."

Another Liberator limped to a field in Sicily, landed without brakes, and coasted into seven American P-40 fighters parked beyond the end of the runway. No one was hurt, but the bomber crew got a very chilly welcome. "We just got finished taking fifteen crackups apart to make these good airplanes," a mechanic snarled at them, "and you guys come along and smash 'em all up."

Stragglers continued to fall by the wayside. Some landed in neutral Turkey and their crews were interned. Others splashed into the sea as fuel gave out. Two Liberators collided in a cloud bank over Bulgaria.

Perhaps the cruelest experience of all was that of a dozen battered B-24s that had managed to get halfway home when they were attacked off the coast of Greece by ten ME-109s. In their first two passes the Messerschmitts knocked down two bombers and lost one of their own number. In the ensuing free-for-all, another Liberator and a German fighter crashed into the sea. Finally the ME-109s turned back, short of fuel.

It was late afternoon before the first Tidal Wave planes arrived back at Benghazi. As they landed, Colonel Smart and other planners learned with horror what had happened to their beautiful scheme. Most of the fliers were too stunned or exhausted to make much sense. The officers sent them off to bed and sat down to await the late arrivals. In the gathering darkness bombers continued to come in, many so badly damaged that ground crews simply shook their heads and tagged the planes for scrapping.

Hours before, far out over the Mediterranean, the number one and two engines of *Liberty Lad* had sputtered out for lack of gasoline. With two engines gone, both on the same wing, the pilot and copilot applied full right rudder to keep the ship airborne. Neither dared relax the pressure on the rudder pedals; crewmen braced the pilots and massaged their stiffening legs.

For four agonizing hours *Liberty Lad* continued to mush along. It was fully dark when the plane reached Benghazi. Brakeless, the B-24 bounced and rolled for a mile before it lurched to a stop. The last of the Tidal Wave force to land, *Liberty Lad* had been in the air sixteen hours.

It was some time before all the details of the Battle of Ploesti could be assembled. The final toll was shocking. Of the 165 Liberators that bombed the refineries, 53 never got back to Benghazi. Nearly a third of the crewmen were dead, wounded, captured, or interned.

As for Ploesti, even though its refineries were severely damaged, they were soon delivering as much fuel as they had been before the raid. The supreme irony of Operation Tidal Wave was that Ploesti was operating at only 60 per cent of its capacity

Their faces reflecting shock and exhaustion, survivors of the Ploesti strike try to answer the questions of intelligence officers at Benghazi. The man at left describes an attack by a German fighter.

when the bombers struck. It was the 40 per cent "cushion" that they had destroyed.

Still, the August 1 raid eventually helped push the Third Reich toward defeat. As oil supplies elsewhere were destroyed by the continuing Allied bomber offensive, Hitler could not call on Ploesti for increased output. The vital reserve capacity he counted on had gone up in flame and smoke under the assault of the low-flying Liberators.

Whether the result was worth the cost is a point still debated. The men of Operation Tidal Wave would never forget the cost. Sitting in the interrogation hut at Benghazi, fresh from his ordeal, one of the Ploesti raiders was asked for his impression of the mission. "We were dragged through the mouth of hell," he said.

5

THE AUTUMN CRISIS

The savage mauling of the Ploesti raiders was not an isolated incident. Barely two weeks later the Luftwaffe delivered a second staggering blow at the AAF. Thus began the autumn crisis of the American daylight bombing offensive.

During the summer of 1943 the Eighth Air Force became at last a real threat to the Third Reich. A few months before, the Eighth had been strained to its limits to send off as many as 100 bombers; now raids three times that size were possible.

With this new strength went a new plan, Operation Pointblank. Pointblank's objective was to so batter Nazi power from the air that an Allied invasion across the English Channel, scheduled for the spring of 1944, could be launched with a better than even chance of success. By night the RAF would continue its attacks on German industrial centers. By day the Americans would concentrate on the Luftwaffe, both on the ground and in combat, in an attempt to seize control of the air over the Continent.

In June, July, and early August the U.S. bombers struck at German aircraft engine and fighter assembly plants, rubber factories (which made,

B-17s fly over the Alps after bombing aircraft factories at Regensburg on August 17, 1943. They landed in North Africa instead of returning to England. This painting hung in a London building damaged by a German V–1 flying bomb in 1944. A bomb fragment made the tear between the planes at left.

77

among other things, airplane tires), and at airfields in occupied France. On August 13 the Liberators that had survived the Ploesti raid pounded an ME-109 factory in Austria.

The Eighth Air Force unleashed its full power to celebrate the first anniversary of its entry into the air war. On August 17, 1943, exactly one year after the Eighth had sent 12 Flying Fortresses to bomb the rail yards at Rouen, it put into the air 376 B-17s to attack the ball bearing plants at Schweinfurt and the Messerschmitt factory at Regensburg. Never before had the Eighth penetrated so deeply into Germany. Never before had it dispatched so many bombers. And never before had the Luftwaffe reacted so violently.

In selecting these two targets the American planning staff was going for the vitals of Hitler's empire. Regensburg assembled about one-third of the Luftwaffe's ME-109 fighters and its destruction would cut deeply into the power of Goering's air force.

The destruction of Schweinfurt might not affect the course of the air war so quickly, but in the long run it might pay far greater dividends. For Schweinfurt, like Ploesti, was essential to the whole German war effort. Everything from field artillery and precision instruments to airplane engines required ball bearings; the German war machine quite literally rolled on them. About half of these bearings were manufactured in Schweinfurt.

The Eighth dipped into its bag of tricks in planning the double mission. The Regensburg force of 146 B-17s was to take off first, along with American P-47 Thunderbolt fighters to provide escort as far as their limited range allowed. It was hoped that the German fighters would concentrate on this force. To give the bomber crews better odds, the planners decided to have them turn south after hitting Regensburg and land in North Africa rather than try to fight their way back to England. The Fortresses were equipped with extra fuel tanks, and the startled fliers were ordered to pack their toothbrushes.

The Regensburg force was, in effect, a smoke screen for the second part of the day's mission. The 230-plane Schweinfurt force, coming along about fifteen minutes later, was supposed to be able to slip through the defenses while the Luftwaffe was busy at Regensburg. It was a sound enough plan, but to work, its timing needed to be exactly right.

On the morning of August 17 fog covered much of England. Yet the weather was clear over the Continent. Fog or no fog, the Regensburg strike was sent off at 8 A.M. in order to reach North Africa before dark. It was decided to hold the takeoff time of the Schweinfurt raiders until 11:30, to give the escort fighters enough time to return from the Continent, refuel, and go out with them. The Luftwaffe made good use of this gift of time.

Lieutenant Colonel Beirne Lay, a copilot on the Regensburg mission,

These scenes were painted in England by Peter Hurd. Above, a B-17 soars over the crumbling battlements of an ancient English castle. Below is the view from the navigator's window of a Flying Fortress.

Daylight precision bombing at its best: bombs of the first wave of Fortresses over Regensburg explode in a tight, deadly pattern on the Messerschmitt aircraft factory. Most of the parked fighters visible on the airfield at lower center were destroyed or damaged.

described the vicious air battle that began soon after the first wave of B-17s crossed the enemy coast. "Two FW-190s appeared at one o'clock level," he wrote, "and whizzed through the formation ahead of us in a frontal attack, nicking two B-17s in the wings and breaking away beneath us in half rolls. . . . The crew sensed trouble. There was something desperate about the way those two fighters came in fast, right out of their climb, without any preliminaries."

The action became more furious by the minute, especially after the U.S. Thunderbolts had to turn back. Colonel Lay remembered seeing "two whole squadrons, twelve ME-109s and eleven FW-190s, climbing parallel to us. . . . Several thousand feet below us were many more fighters, with their noses cocked at maximum climb. Over the interphone came reports of an equal number of enemy aircraft deploying on the other side."

He was amazed at the litter of battle. The sky seemed filled with burning bombers and exploding fighters, with parachutes and bodies and pieces of planes. He watched a B-17 sag out of formation with its cockpit on fire: "The copilot crawled out of his window, held on with one hand, reached back for his chute, buckled it on, let go, and was whisked back into the horizontal stabilizer. I believe the impact killed him. His chute didn't open." Another Fortress blew up with a blinding flash as its bomb load was touched off, raining debris and four

balls of fire that had been the gas tanks.

For an hour and a half the attacks continued without letup. Luftwaffe spotter planes flew alongside the bomber formations, co-ordinating the fighters' tactics. "The manner of their attacks," Colonel Lay wrote, "showed that some pilots were old-timers, some amateurs, and that all knew pretty definitely where we were going and were inspired with a fanatical determination to stop us before we got there." He noted that veteran German pilots made their frontal assaults at a slower rate of speed to make sure they scored hits; the beginners slammed through the formations full throttle, shooting wildly.

Just before the bombers reached Regensburg the fighters faded away, apparently regrouping to make new attacks. The battered force made its bombing run relatively free of opposition. The bombing was exceptionally accurate, hitting nearly every building in the huge Messerschmitt works and demolishing dozens of completed fighters parked ready for delivery to Luftwaffe combat squadrons.

The turn toward North Africa rather than back to England surprised the enemy, and fighters caused little more trouble. A few crippled Fortresses landed in neutral Switzerland. Others limped on across the Alps only to crash into the Mediterranean, unable to stretch their fuel supply to reach the far shore. All told, 24 out of the 146 bombers were lost. It was dusk when the survivors landed in

The Luftwaffe threw its heaviest weapons into the autumn air battles in 1943. The ME-109 above is armed with eight-inch rockets in underwing tubes. The Messerschmitt at right carries a bomb and mounts a powerful cannon firing through the propeller hub.

Algeria. "We felt the reaction of men who had not expected to see another sunset," Colonel Lay wrote.

Meanwhile, the force bound for Schweinfurt was suffering just as heavily. Trailing the Regensburg strike not by fifteen minutes, but by some three and a half hours, and following the same course most of the way, it found the enemy ready and waiting.

Some German pilots, recalling the air fighting traditions of the First World War, had painted their fighters in an exotic fashion. There were Messerschmitts with yellow noses and red propeller spinners; Focke-Wulfs with one wing painted white, the other black; even fighters in zebra stripes or checkerboard patterns. The fighters trailed the B-17s all the way to Schweinfurt and all the way back to the French coast. Only the arrival of RAF Spitfires at that point kept the battle from continuing out over the English Channel.

Thirty-six of the Flying Fortresses that struck Schweinfurt failed to return, bringing the total losses on August 17 to 60. German losses are not known precisely; although 288 fighters were claimed by American gun-

BOTH: ARCHIV KRUEGER

ners, the actual score was certainly a great deal lower because of the duplication of claims. The Luftwaffe's high command had reason to be pleased with the day's results. Each bomber that fell took ten Americans out of the war. But each ME-109 or FW-190 shot down carried only one man—and many fighter pilots parachuted safely and lived to fight another day.

The bombing of the ball bearing plants had been accurate and damaging, but another raid was necessary to complete the destruction. The Eighth Air Force began preparations for a second visit to Schweinfurt.

A spell of bad weather in September frustrated the Eighth's plans. The bombers were able to hit German tar-

gets only twice during the month, and one of those raids cost 45 planes. In October the weather improved, and the Eighth stepped up its offensive. The result was what an air force historian has called "the critical week" in the American air war against Nazi Germany.

On October 8 the cities of Bremen and Vegesack were raided and 30 bombers were lost. The next day aircraft factories on the German Baltic coast were the targets, and 28 planes failed to return. On October 10 Münster was attacked, at a cost of another 30 bombers. Then, on October 14, there occurred one of the greatest battles in the history of aerial warfare. Once more the target was Schweinfurt.

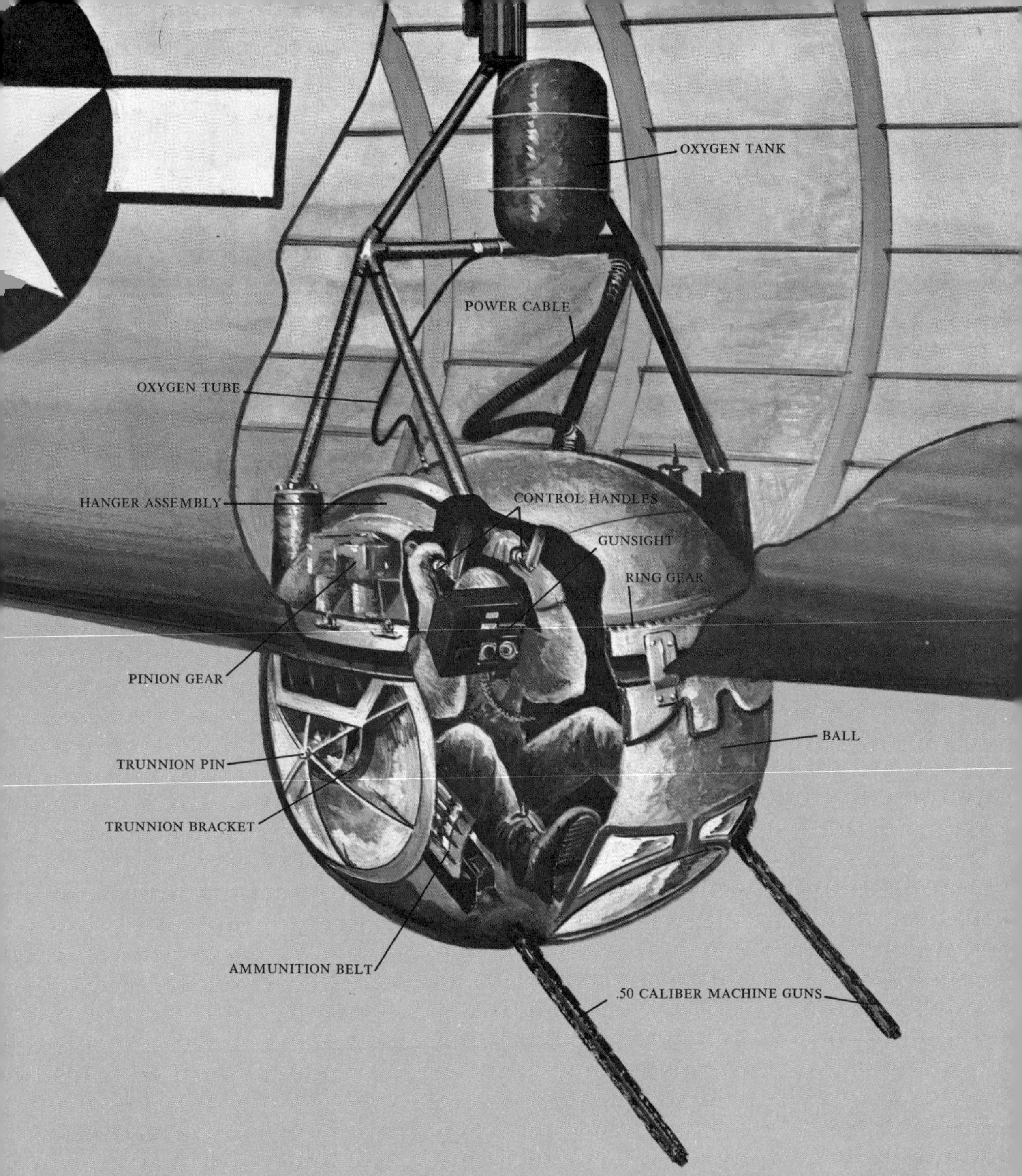

OXYGEN TANK

POWER CABLE

OXYGEN TUBE

HANGER ASSEMBLY

CONTROL HANDLES

GUNSIGHT

RING GEAR

PINION GEAR

BALL

TRUNNION PIN

TRUNNION BRACKET

AMMUNITION BELT

.50 CALIBER MACHINE GUNS

This cutaway view shows the B-17's Sperry ball turret. The BALL *and its fixed guns turned up or down on two* TRUNNION PINS *mounted in* TRUNNION BRACKETS. *The brackets were part of the* HANGER ASSEMBLY *supporting the ball. When a power-operated* PINION GEAR *in the hanger assembly meshed with a* RING GEAR *bolted to the floor of the B-17, the hanger assembly and ball revolved horizontally. The gunner gripped two* CONTROL HANDLES. *Moving them from side to side turned the ball right or left; moving them vertically rotated the ball up or down. He fired his guns by pressing buttons on the handles. The* GUNSIGHT *computed just how much to "lead" an attacking fighter. The gunner maneuvered the ball to keep the fighter framed in the gunsight, adjusted the sight with a foot pedal, and opened fire.*

In a drizzle, under low, leaden clouds, 323 Flying Fortresses and 60 Liberators took off that morning. They had to climb more than a mile before they broke out into sunlight, and in the process the Liberators failed to assemble properly. All 60 had to abort the mission. Thirty-two B-17s soon returned because of mechanical failures. Thus, even before crossing the enemy coast, the Schweinfurt attackers had lost a quarter of their strength.

A swarm of Thunderbolt escorts helped to blunt the early German fighter attacks. With extra gas tanks slung under their fuselages to increase range, the P-47s stayed with the bombers as far as the German border; then, with 13 enemy fighters to their credit, they had to wheel around and head back to England. Freed of these pests, the German pilots lined up to take cracks at the Flying Fortresses.

The group commander who insisted that he saw the entire German Air Force during the three-hour Battle of Schweinfurt was not exaggerating very much. It seemed that anything that could carry a gun or a bomb or a rocket was in the air. Most were single-engine ME-109s and FW-190s, but there were scores of twin-engine Messerschmitts and Junkers 88s. American fliers spotted outdated German bombers of the type that were slaughtered in the Battle of Britain back in 1940; there were even several Stuka dive bombers, looking very out of place at a height of four miles.

To many bomber crewmen there was an unreal quality about the tense moments before the engagement. The sky was a brilliant, sun-washed blue, peaceful and unmarked by any trace of battle. The only sounds were the muted thunder of the engines and occasional comments on the interphone. Then the enemy appeared: a tightly grouped covey of gleaming, polished Focke-Wulf 190s rising off to one side as if they were on an express elevator, the sun glinting on their propellers and turning them into flashing disks. The fighters slid effortlessly ahead of the bombers and grew small in the distance. Then, still in perfect formation, they peeled off in groups of four and grew large again with terrifying speed. In only seconds they were close enough to open fire. Their wings and engine cowlings sparkled brightly. Now the unreality was gone, replaced by an unholy din.

The B-17s' nose and top turret guns stuttered and pounded. Their tracers reached out and crossed those of the incoming fighters. Strings of white puffs appeared magically around the bombers as the enemy cannon shells exploded. The Focke-Wulfs flipped over and down, presenting a brief glimpse of armored belly to the gunners, and with a high-pitched screech were gone. Hardly had they passed from view when a second flight of fighters raced in, then a third and a fourth, as if a movie projector had gone out of kilter and kept showing the same film over and over again.

During the first moments of battle the American gunners tended to shoot wildly, pouring out long, wasteful bursts of fire, yelling their sightings into the interphones. But as the assaults continued they settled down to their grim business more professionally. They tracked the fighters carefully and shortened their bursts, calmly calling off new attacks.

Gunners recalled later that they had never been so busy as they were the day of the Schweinfurt mission. To meet head-on attacks the bombardier and the navigator of a B-17 had three machine guns—one in the plexiglass nose, one mounted farther back in each side wall—and they had to jump back and forth between them.

The top turret gunner, standing directly behind the cockpit with his head and shoulders wedged into the turret, had a much wider range of fire. His turret revolved hydraulically, and his twin guns could be elevated from horizontal to vertical. While he defended against frontal attacks he also had to be alert for German fighters swooping down from directly above. The radio compartment, aft of the top turret, had a single machine gun mounted in the roof; although his field of fire was limited, the radioman provided extra insurance against attacks from above.

Without doubt the most uncomfortable station in a Flying Fortress was that of the ball turret gunner. Curled up within the tiny metal and plexiglass

ball set in the bottom of the plane, he spun himself about at a dizzy pace to bring his twin guns to bear on a speeding fighter.

Still farther aft were the two waist gunners, standing at their open windows in the biting wind to work their single guns. On this day, October 14, there were few waist gunners who were not ankle-deep in empty shell casings before the battle was an hour old.

At the very rear of the ship was the tail gunner, who crouched on his knees to operate his twin guns. Under certain conditions the tail gunner had an extra hazard to worry about. If the combination of water vapor and temperature was right, the bombers (and the fighters, as well) emitted swirling white streamers called contrails—water vapor condensed by the turbulent passage of the wings and propellers through the air. German

These photographs, taken during combat, show German rocket-carrying twin-engine fighters in action. At top rockets burst near a B-17 as Messerschmitt 410s (lower left and lower right) make frontal attacks. At center is an ME-110 silhouetted between a pair of B-17s. At bottom, an ME-110 takes a position on the tail of a B-17, a favorite spot from which to fire heavy rockets.

OVERLEAF: *Ball bearing plants in Schweinfurt burn under the assault of U.S. B-17s. The two raids on Schweinfurt in August and October of 1943 "evoked a crisis," according to the head of German war production. But the battered Eighth Air Force was not able to deliver a third attack until four months later; by then the Germans had recovered and the bearing crisis had passed.*

U.S. AIR FORCE

twin-engine fighters often sneaked up unseen behind a bomber formation under cover of these contrails to release their deadly rockets.

The key to a bomber's defense was co-ordination between every member of the crew. By skidding the plane slightly to right or left, a good pilot could "uncover" more of his guns to meet an attacker. By calling off the direction an enemy pilot took when he broke away after firing, the men manning the nose guns alerted the ball turret gunner or the tail gunner for a quick shot as the fighters whizzed past. The copilot, too, was busy. He checked battle damage, gave first aid to wounded crewmen, or helped the pilot hold a damaged ship in formation—for it often took brute strength to fight the controls of a crippled bomber.

A crewman badly hit by a German bullet or shell had little chance to survive unless he was given first aid immediately. In the thin, frigid air above 20,000 feet medical treatment was no easy task. Oxygen was often the first need; anyone cut off from his supply collapsed within minutes. The cold, too, was a mortal enemy. A co-pilot removing his gloves to apply a tourniquet to a gunner whose leg had been blown off by a cannon shell had only a minute or two to work before

his hands became numb and useless.

No matter how serious his troubles —crewmen dead or wounded, an engine shot out, the nose of the plane blown open by a cannon shell—the pilot fought desperately to stay with the massed defensive fire of the formation. A straggler was as good as lost. The enemy gave no quarter; whenever a B-17 dropped out of formation the fighters pounced on it to administer the killing volley.

The Luftwaffe sprang no new tricks on the Schweinfurt raiders, but never before had it combined all its tactics so skillfully.

German pilots attacked out of the sun, making themselves virtually impossible to see. They tried air-to-air bombing or dropped parachute bombs that floated down into the formations and exploded. They concentrated on the lead bombers in each formation, and on the top and bottom groups. At the same time as flights of ME-109s and FW-190s launched frontal attacks with rockets and cannon shells, other fighters struck from above or below or from the sides or the rear. Screened by the swift interceptors, twin-engine fighters slipped in close to release their heavy rockets.

These rockets, which traveled slowly enough to be clearly visible, were an especially chilling sight to the American fliers. One of the bomber pilots flying the Schweinfurt mission watched in horror as a rocket arched through his formation, heading straight for a

An AAF cameraman taking routine bomb-drop pictures over Germany recorded instead this freak accident. Just as the Fortress released its bombs, another Fortress flew directly into their path. The mangled B-17 fell out of control and its crew bailed out.

nearby B-17. It hit the fuselage just back of the cockpit, tearing open the side of the plane and blowing one wing completely off. The pilot briefly glimpsed the men in the cockpit still sitting at their controls; then they were engulfed in flames.

A Flying Fortress did not always die so quickly. It became commonplace to see a big bomber drift back from one formation to another with one or two engines stopped, until at last it faded from sight far astern, surrounded by a swarm of German planes.

The enemy, too, suffered heavily. One moment a fighter curved gracefully across the sky; the next moment it was gone in a brilliant flash as bullets found its gas tanks. Others cartwheeled crazily as a wing broke off, or fell straight down completely enveloped in flames. Far below, the course of the Battle of Schweinfurt could be traced by the plumes of oily smoke rising from bombers and fighters that had plunged into the ground.

The approach to the target cost the Eighth Air Force 28 bombers, and 34 others turned back with mechanical failures or battle damage. By the time Schweinfurt was reached there were but 229 B-17s left. Still the German pilots bored in, paying no attention to their own flak.

It took twelve minutes for the bombers to release almost 500 tons of bombs on the ball bearing plants. A bombardier remembered how "the smoke rolled up, then there was a big explosion and all of a sudden there was a great splash of fire right in the center of everything."

As the bombers struggled back toward England, the Luftwaffe redoubled its efforts. By this time many fighter squadrons had landed for more gas and ammunition and returned to the battle. Bad weather over the British Isles prevented friendly fighters from meeting the returning formations, and so the German pilots continued the pursuit far out over the English Channel. Thirty-two more Fortresses were lost on the return flight.

None of these B-17s died more stubbornly than one named *Brennan's Circus*. Its ordeal had begun half an hour before the target was reached. A pair of ME-109s attacking from the rear riddled the fuselage and wings with cannon shells and shot out one engine. The radioman got one of the Messerschmitts in his sights and blew it up. The enemy swarmed in for the kill.

The ball turret gunner set a Focke-Wulf on fire; the two waist gunners each claimed a fighter. In the meantime, however, the B-17's speed had dropped sharply, ending any chance of staying with the protecting guns of the formation. The pilot elected to dive down to the ground and try to sneak away safely a few feet above the treetops. A second engine was knocked out on the way down. For a while the fighters continued to pelt the battered Fortress with bullets and shells, but pressing home attacks so near the ground was hazardous and they finally gave up.

The smoking bomber now became the target of ground fire. "They were firing machine guns and everything else," one of the gunners said. "Troops were lined up on rooftops and in the streets and fields, blazing away with rifles. Their officers also were outside, firing pistols. If they'd had more time, they probably would have

This Flying Fortress brought a dead ball turret gunner back from a mission over Germany. The flak shell that killed him burst with such murderous force that it bent one of the turret's guns. Although flak knocked down far fewer bombers than did enemy fighters, the American crewmen hated flak more, because they had no way to fight back at the antiaircraft gunners on the ground.

thrown rocks at us." Just as *Brennan's Circus* crossed the enemy coast a third engine died.

A B-17 was not really supposed to be able to fly on one engine, but this one did—at least for a while. The laboring motor carried *Brennan's Circus* within a few miles of the English coast before the laws of aerodynamics finally caught up with it. The pilot skillfully ditched the bomber in the Channel; it floated long enough for the crewmen to get into their life rafts, and an hour later a British launch rescued them.

American combat losses on the Schweinfurt mission totaled 65 Flying Fortresses: 59 shot down over Europe, *Brennan's Circus* lost in the Channel, and five more destroyed attempting to land or, too badly damaged to land, abandoned in the air over England. A further 17 proved impossible to repair and were scrapped.

Some units were all but wiped out; one bomber group, for instance, lost 13 of the 15 Flying Fortresses that had set out across the enemy coast. The human toll was 642 fliers killed, captured or wounded. All told, October 14, 1943, was the worst day in the history of the Eighth Air Force.

To make matters worse, this sacrifice of lives was largely in vain. Schweinfurt's factories, although once more badly damaged, were not destroyed. The Germans immediately

began to move bearing-making machinery to other, safer locations. Attacks on Schweinfurt were resumed in 1944, but Nazi leaders could boast at the end of the war that their output of weapons was never once delayed because of a shortage of bearings.

Schweinfurt was the climax of a terrible week—153 heavy bombers lost in seven days. It symbolized, as well, the critical condition of the whole American daylight bombing campaign. The Luftwaffe had won the autumn battle decisively.

Even as the Eighth Air Force reeled under the hammer blows of the Luftwaffe, the RAF was putting the finishing touches on its plan to do to Berlin what had been done to Hamburg. "We can wreck Berlin from end to end," wrote the head of the RAF's Bomber Command, "if the AAF will come in on it. It will cost between 400–500 aircraft. It will cost Germany the war." The AAF, however, could not "come in on it." It had been stopped cold. As the British had warned, heavy bombers could not steadily attack the heart of the Third Reich in daylight without fighter escort.

And yet, four months after the Schweinfurt disaster, the Eighth Air Force resumed major daylight strikes against targets deep inside Nazi Germany. This comeback was due to two inventions. The first was a simple gasoline container called a drop-tank; the second was a remarkable long-range fighter plane called the Mustang.

These sketches of wounded bomber crewmen are by war artist Lawrence Smith. The man at top receives first aid inside the plane. At the left, a casualty is placed on a stretcher while the other members of his crew look on.

6

"LITTLE FRIENDS"

The creation of the P-51 Mustang is one of the curious ironies of the European air war. The British insisted that American daylight bombing could not succeed; yet the British were behind the design of the fighter plane that led the way to its final success.

For a time a long-range escort fighter appeared impossible to build. The British had the Spitfire, and the Germans had the Messerschmitt 109 and the Focke-Wulf 190; all three were excellent fighters, but none of them could escort bombers for much more than 250 miles. They were best suited to defense. The trick was to design a truly offensive fighter to escort bombers 500 or 600 or 700 miles to the target, meet enemy fighters there on equal terms, and then shepherd the bombers home again; in other words, what was needed was a plane with the range of a bomber and the performance of a fighter. Twin-engine fighters were able to carry enough gasoline for the long trip, but they could not stand up to more agile single-engine interceptors.

In the spring of 1940 the British approached North American Avia-

A Mustang nicknamed Shangri-La, *piloted by fighter ace Don Gentile, prepares to take off on a mission over Germany in 1944. The two wing drop-tanks enabled the P-51 to escort bombers into any corner of the Third Reich. On this mission Gentile shot down three Luftwaffe fighters. He ended up with a total of 30 victories: 23 in aerial combat and seven in strafing attacks on airfields.*

97

tion, a small California firm best known as the builder of a widely used training plane. The RAF wanted to place an order for P-40 Warhawk ground-attack fighters. North American suggested instead an entirely new fighter. The British agreed to the idea —if the design could be completed within 120 days. (The RAF was in a desperate hurry for combat planes in those grim days of 1940.)

North American's designers closeted themselves in a room in the company's plant in Inglewood, California, and set to work. One of the engineers recalled that "the Mustang materialized out of that smoke-filled room where men knew no hours, where lights never went out; where for days all you could hear was the rattle of paper, the sharpening of pencils, and the noise of men knocking out their pipes on waste baskets."

Airplane designers of that time could choose between two types of piston engines, radial or in-line. The cylinders of a radial engine were arranged like the spokes of a wheel around a short crankshaft. This type was powerful and had the advantage of being air-cooled, but it also had a major drawback—its large frontal area meant a blunt-nosed fighter that butted its way through the air rather than sliding through it. The German designer Kurt Tank had done a masterful job of reducing this frontal drag problem in his radial-engined Focke-Wulf 190, but there were not many designers with Tank's ability.

*Above, fighter ace Robert Johnson (28 victories) and a ground crew-
man check a Thunderbolt's guns. Below the guns is the mount for a
drop-tank. The picture sequence on the opposite page was taken by
the gun camera of a U.S. fighter. As the American pilot's bullets
strike the underside of the Focke-Wulf, the German flier climbs out
of his cockpit (top) and then tumbles away from his burning plane.*

99

These pictures show the two types of engines used in AAF fighters. The mechanics above service a Mustang's Rolls-Royce in-line engine. The man at the left loads a belt of .50 caliber ammunition.

In an in-line engine the cylinders were arranged in rows along a lengthy crankshaft. The small frontal area meant that a fighter designed around an in-line engine could have a sleek, pointed nose to cut down drag. Both the Spitfire and the ME-109 used this type of engine. Its big disadvantage was that it had to be liquid cooled, requiring radiators which were vulnerable to enemy bullets in combat.

The Mustang's designers chose the General Motors Allison in-line engine, for their goal was a clean-lined plane that would squeeze every available mile out of a gallon of gasoline. With this thought in mind they also used a radical new airfoil—the cross-section shape of the wing—that smoothed the flow of air and cut normal wing drag in half.

The first hand-built Mustang was rolled out of a North American hangar in exactly 100 days. Its flight tests delighted the British, and the new fighter went into limited production in 1941. The first one was delivered to Great Britain a month before Pearl Harbor. The RAF considered the P-51 the best American-built fighter then available. Strangely enough, the United States expressed little interest in the Mustang.

Although the U.S. Army Air Force showed great foresight in fighting for the Flying Fortress in the 1930s, it had made the mistake of putting most of its eggs in the bomber basket. Con-

BOTH: U.S. AIR FORCE

Ground crewmen work on a Thunderbolt's 2,000-horsepower Pratt and Whitney radial engine. Equipped with eight machine guns and a ton of bombs or rockets, P-47s were widely used fighter-bombers.

vinced that the B-17s and the B-24s could defend themselves, the AAF made no effort to develop a long-range, single-engine escort fighter. This policy helped bring about the crisis of daylight bombing in 1943.

The AAF was not without fighters, of course. Its best ones were the Lockheed P-38 Lightning and the Republic P-47 Thunderbolt. Both were in action in 1943, and both were unusual planes.

The P-38 had a pair of in-line engines mounted in long, slim booms that also supported the tail. The finest twin-engine fighter of its day, the Lightning was very successful against the Japanese in the Pacific theater, and it served gallantly in Europe

early in 1944. But it was neither so fast nor so maneuverable as the Luftwaffe interceptors, and was not the really effective escort fighter that the AAF needed.

Republic's radial-engine Thunderbolt was a huge hulk of an airplane, the largest, heaviest, single-engine fighter of the war. It was so big, in fact, that when it first arrived in England RAF fliers commented with straight faces that a P-47 pilot could hop out of his seat and dodge around inside the barrel-like fuselage if the Luftwaffe attacks got too hot. The Thunderbolt might look like a dray horse when set next to a thoroughbred Spitfire or Focke-Wulf, but it was a fierce competitor. It could take

on the best of the German interceptors, proved itself a potent fighter-
bomber for ground attacks, and was
second to none in its ability to absorb punishment and still keep flying.

Robert Johnson, one of the leading
American fighter aces of the war,
testified to the Thunderbolt's ruggedness when, in the summer of 1943, his
squadron was "bounced" by a flight
of FW-190s over France. German
cannon shells smashed into Johnson's
P-47. The cockpit canopy was shattered, the instrument panel wrecked,
and the engine began to smoke, leak
oil, and clank ominously. The wings
and tail looked like Swiss cheese.

Nearly blinded by spraying hydrau-
lic fluid, Johnson's first thought was
to bail out. But a cannon shell had
jammed the canopy frame; try as he
might he could not get it open far
enough to crawl out. He had no
choice but to try and nurse the P-47
back to England.

As he limped across the French
coast he found unwelcome company
—a sleek, yellow-nosed Focke-Wulf
190 from one of the Luftwaffe's crack
fighter squadrons. Three times the
Focke-Wulf pilot planted himself on
Johnson's tail and raked his plane
with machine gun bullets—the German had apparently used up all his
cannon ammunition in the recent air

*Quick recognition of friend and foe was one
of the fighter pilot's problems, but no one
had any trouble identifying the distinctive
shape of P-38 Lightnings, pictured here in
formation over France. The Germans called
the American fighter the "fork-tailed devil."*

battle. After each pass he flew close
alongside the riddled and helpless
Thunderbolt, shaking his head at its
condition. Finally, far out over the
English Channel, the enemy pilot
rocked his wings in an admiring salute
and curved away toward home.

Johnson skillfully landed the brakeless P-47 at his base. He counted 21
cannon-shell holes in the plane, and
gave up trying to count the number of
bullet holes. The Thunderbolt had to
be scrapped.

The P-47 had everything—speed,
ruggedness, maneuverability, a powerful eight-gun punch—everything but
range. It was here that the drop-tank
entered the picture. A tank holding
108 gallons of gasoline had been developed by early 1943, but because of
exasperating production delays it did
not become available until fall. This
belly tank increased the Thunderbolt's range by more than fifty per
cent; when it was empty, or if enemy
planes appeared, the pilot dropped the
tank and was ready to fight. Soon
wing tanks were in production to ex-
tend the P-47's range further.

As for the Mustang, the AAF had
taken a long second look at the idea
of adding the new fighter to the American arsenal. Its decision was made a
good deal easier by a brilliant stroke
of British-American co-operation.
Major Thomas Hitchcock, an American military aide stationed in England, had followed the Mustang's development closely. At his suggestion,
the Allison engine was replaced by a

*Crewmen of an Eighth Air Force B-17 head for a celebration mark-
ing the end of their tour of combat duty (25 missions) early in 1944.
Left to right are the pilot, bombardier, navigator, top turret gunner,
radioman, the waist gunners with their guns, and the tail gunner.*

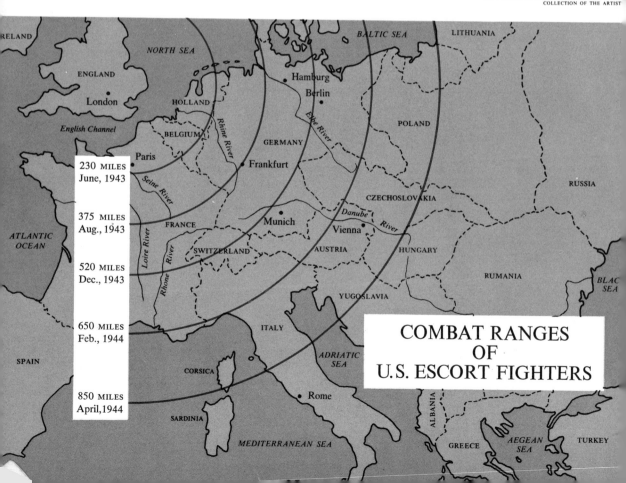

230 MILES
June, 1943

375 MILES
Aug., 1943

520 MILES
Dec., 1943

650 MILES
Feb., 1944

850 MILES
April, 1944

COMBAT RANGES
OF
U.S. ESCORT FIGHTERS

more powerful Rolls-Royce Merlin of the type used in the RAF's Spitfire.

The improvement was sensational. The Merlin boosted the P-51's speed to more than 440 miles per hour, making it faster than any standard Luftwaffe fighter. It was also more maneuverable, and its long range was not affected by the new engine. Arrangements were made to manufacture the Merlin in the United States, assembly lines were set up, and in 1943 the Mustang went into full production.

Despite disasters like Schweinfurt, the leaders of the American bombing campaign were optimistic as 1943 drew to a close. New bombers and crews arrived to replace those lost in the autumn air battles. Escort fighters —Lightnings, Thunderbolts mounting drop-tanks, and a few Mustangs—became available. And a new command setup went into effect. General Spaatz took control of the U.S. strategic air campaign; the Eighth Air Force went to General Jimmy Doolittle; and General Eaker assumed command of the Allied air forces in the Mediterranean theater. Under Eaker was the

John McCoy's painting at top shows Mustangs of the 4th Fighter Group. The 4th claimed 1,016 German planes, the top score of any U.S. fighter group. The map at left illustrates the growing effectiveness of fighter cover for the bombers. The 230-mile range of the Thunderbolt was increased in August, 1943, by a belly tank. In December Lightnings with 75-gallon wing tanks arrived. After February, 1944, Mustangs with 75-gallon wing tanks could fly all the way to Berlin. Finally, the P-51's range was increased to 850 miles by larger wing tanks.

new U.S. Fifteenth Air Force, ready to join the assault on Germany from its recently captured bases in Italy.

Then the weather refused to cooperate. The AAF was ready to strike again at the heart of the Third Reich by December, but it was not until mid-February of 1944 that it could get into high gear.

During these winter months of bad weather, efforts were made at electronic bombing. The bombers were equipped with radar sets that gave an outline picture of the target city even though the ground was obscured by clouds. The results, however, were disappointing. Bombing accuracy was usually bad, and German war production suffered little. About all that could be said for radar bombing was that it was better than no bombing at all.

On December 13, 1943, Mustangs flew their first escort mission to the Third Reich. Several more times that month German interceptors found American fighters waiting for them when they attacked the bomber formations. On January 11, 1944, the Eighth Air Force tried to return to its main target, the Luftwaffe, by bombing aircraft factories deep within Germany. Although the U.S. escort fighters put up a stiff battle—the 49 Mustangs claimed 15 of the enemy without losing a plane—there were far too few of them. Sixty of the 651 bombers were knocked down.

There may not have been enough of these escort fighters yet, but those

107

The North American P-51 is considered to be the finest all-around fighter plane of World War II. As this painting shows, the Mustang was considerably different from its chief opponent, the FW-190. Its 1,450 horsepower Rolls-Royce engine gave a top speed of 440 miles per hour. Air entering a scoop under the fuselage cooled the radiator (visible above and behind the air scoop) needed by the in-line engine. Behind the pilot is the radio; farther aft are yellow oxygen tanks. Three fuel tanks—one behind the cockpit and one in each wing—gave the Mustang exceptional range. Because of the wing fuel tanks there was no room for heavy cannon; but since the P-51 was to fight fighters rather than bombers, its six machine guns were adequate. Ammunition belts are next to the guns. The P-51D version shown here had a bubble canopy to increase the pilot's visibility.

that did appear gave a tremendous boost to the morale of the bomber crewmen. These men were required to fly 25 combat missions, and for a time in the fall of 1943 the odds against their completing a tour of duty were frightening to think about. They felt very much alone and very close to death as the enemy swarmed in from every direction. Now, at last, there was help. Escort fighters were a welcome sight, and the bomber crews called them "Little Friends." Perhaps a tail gunner said it best when he remarked, "Every time I see a P-51, I want to go up and shake his hand."

The tide of the air war finally turned in favor of the AAF during a seven-day period in February of 1944. Forecasters predicted a stretch of good weather, and the AAF and the RAF threw every plane they had into the battle. Time was running short. The cross-Channel invasion was now less than four months away, and the Luftwaffe was nowhere near defeated.

The so-called "Big Week" began on the night of February 19 with a heavy RAF raid on Leipzig. In rapid-fire order came a parade of massive American and British attacks. By the end of the Big Week over 2,300 RAF bombers and 3,800 AAF bombers—500 of them flying from the Fifteenth Air Force's bases in Italy—had pounded German aircraft plants, airfields, and ball bearing factories. More than 3,600 fighter sorties, or

The P-51s above are trucked through the streets of an English port after having been shipped across the Atlantic on the deck of a freighter. At right, an RAF airman sitting on a captured ME-109 explains the fighter's strong and weak points to U.S. fliers. Behind him is an FW-190.

missions, were flown in support of the big bombers. Nearly 20,000 tons of bombs fell on the Third Reich that week.

This immense effort had a vital effect on the course of the air war. The German aircraft industry was battered badly enough to lose two months' production—exactly as if it had shut down for that length of time—and this loss came just at the moment that the Luftwaffe was desperately trying to marshal its forces to meet the expected invasion. Yet German losses on the airfields and in the factories were not what made the Big Week so big; it was what took place in the air that was crucial.

Some 450 Nazi fighters were shot down during the Big Week. The Luftwaffe simply could not afford such losses. The planes could eventually be replaced, but the mounting loss of pilots was a mortal blow. To train a fighter pilot took months; to be truly effective he needed considerable experience in combat. In February, 1944, Hermann Goering's Luftwaffe began to lose control of the air over its homeland.

The diary of German fighter pilot Heinz Knoke gives a vivid picture of the Luftwaffe's dilemma. On February 21, early in the Big Week, he told of flying two missions: "We had orders to draw off the escorting fighters

at any cost and to keep them engaged in combat with us. Other squadrons meanwhile attacked the heavy bombers. That cost my squadron two more dead." Two missions were flown the next day: "I do not have a chance to fire at any of the bombers because I have to spend half an hour in a dogfight with a whole pack of Thunderbolts."

February 24: "The squadron loses another six killed at noon today in a dogfight with Thunderbolts, Lightnings, and Mustangs covering another heavy bombing attack. Our little band grows smaller and smaller. Every man can work out for himself on the fingers of one hand when his own turn is due to come." February 25: "The Americans and British conduct their large-scale air operations in a way which leaves us no respite. . . . Night after night the wail of the sirens heralds more raids. How much longer can it all continue?"

The AAF scented victory and its blood was up. Mustangs arrived in an ever-increasing stream; fitted with drop-tanks under their wings, the Little Friends could now escort bombers deep into Germany. Wing tanks stretched the combat range of the Thunderbolts to nearly 500 miles. Now the Eighth Air Force was ready at last to attack in daylight a target it had once only dreamed of.

Flares, searchlights, and burning buildings light the night sky over Berlin in this German painting. In the winter of 1943–44, the RAF tried, but failed, to destroy Berlin as it had destroyed Hamburg.

On March 4 U.S. bombers struck for the first time at Berlin, one of four great raids that month on the capital of Hitler's Third Reich. The first raid surprised the Luftwaffe, and fighter opposition was light. After that, however, the enemy interceptors reacted furiously.

In desperation the Luftwaffe took to attacking the vast bomber formations with formations of its own, the Focke-Wulfs and Messerschmitts escorting heavily armed, twin-engine "bomber destroyers." Into this massed force plunged the U.S. fighters. An American pilot described one of these March air battles as "a great big rat race. There was absolutely no room in that sky for everyone, all with wide-open engines, all guns firing."

The stream of bombers, hundreds upon hundreds of them, stretched as far as the eye could see. Darting around and through this vast armada were the fighters, both friend and foe. The sky was pock-marked with flak and crisscrossed with the fire of thousands of machine guns and cannon and rockets. As the swirling battle moved ponderously across Germany, it trailed bits and pieces of wreckage —burning bombers, swaying parachutes, fighters careening out of control.

These four Berlin raids cost the Eighth Air Force 132 bombers, but the Luftwaffe was being beaten to death. Its strength dwindled away; as the spring wore on, the change was dramatic. Less and less often did its

fighters rise to oppose the attacking bomber formations.

The Luftwaffe lost control of the air in the spring of 1944 not only because it was overwhelmed by superior numbers but because it was outflown and outfought by American fighters. The Luftwaffe interceptors were actually hampered by their heavy firepower. Loaded down with ammunition, bombs, and rockets to be used against the bombers, the ME-109s and FW-190s were sluggish and hard to fly in combat with the American escort fighters. As for the bulky bomber destroyers, the U.S. fighters picked them off like ducks in a shooting gallery.

The fighter pilots of both sides faced a never-ending battle against physical exhaustion. German pilots might fly as many as four sorties in one day. American pilots flew less often, but each of their escort missions lasted for hours.

Robert Johnson, the pilot who had such a narrow escape nursing his crippled P-47 back to England, recalled one day in the spring of 1944 when he had to fly two five-hour sorties. "It was really quite a lot," he said, "when you stop and think that my breakfast was a piece of brown bread and peanut butter and a cup of real heavy stuff they called coffee. We came home, had a quick sandwich and a little shot of whiskey, then back in the airplanes and off we'd go again. We'd come home and flop on our beds with our clothes on

Charles Cundall's painting above shows RAF bomber crews waiting for a raid. In the German painting below, a British flier bails out of a burning Stirling bomber as the victor, an FW-190, sweeps past.

and never move until they waked us for another mission early the next morning."

A month or so before the cross-Channel invasion, the heavy bombers concentrated on Western Europe's transportation network to prevent the Germans from moving up reinforcements. Helping to clear the way for the coming assault, Allied fighters strafed the Luftwaffe's bases. In addition, B-17s and B-24s dropped many thousands of tons of bombs on the launching sites of Hitler's new secret weapons: a jet-propelled pilotless flying bomb called the V-1 and a huge ballistic missile known as the V-2.

Even though the heavy bombers were badly used in this case (fighters equipped for dive-bombing were more effective against the small launching sites than high-altitude attacks), the sheer weight of their bombs took a toll. The onslaught of the secret

At left, B-17s bomb Berlin through heavy clouds. An engine of the B-17 at top has been hit and set afire by flak. The German photograph below, showing Hamburg after an RAF raid, was taken on June 6, 1944— the day that Allied forces invaded France.

STUDIO SCHMIDT-LUCHS, HAMBURG

weapons was delayed several months. Had the campaign against them failed, there would have been terrible carnage in the English ports crammed with men and ships and guns. General Dwight Eisenhower, supreme commander of the Allied forces, admitted that the V-1s and V-2s could have made the invasion impossible.

More important even than the tactical victories over the secret weapons and the enemy transportation system, however, was the fact that the American daylight air campaign (with a large helping hand from the RAF night raiders) broke the back of the Luftwaffe. Goering's air force was hardly to be seen over France on D-Day, June 6. So great was Allied air superiority that General Eisenhower could with confidence announce to his forces on the eve of D-Day, "If you see fighting aircraft over you, they will be ours."

Ground crewmen clean and load the guns of a Thunderbolt, readying it for D-Day action. So great was the Allied air superiority over the invasion beaches that only a handful of pilots saw a Luftwaffe plane.

BERT STILES, JR.

Page from a Copilot's Diary

In the spring and summer of 1944 Bert Stiles, Jr., a 23-year-old Eighth Air Force second lieutenant from Denver, Colorado, saw war for the first time. He flew thirty-five combat missions as copilot in a "big bird" (as he called the Flying Fortress), and between missions he wrote about what it was like to fight four or five miles above the earth. In 1952 his book, Serenade to the Big Bird, *was published in the United States by W. W. Norton & Company. The part of the book reprinted below describes a raid on the city of Leipzig, deep inside Germany, not long after D-Day.*

The crews scheduled for the haul were waked up around 3 A.M. There was plenty of grousing about that. I was so tired I felt drunk.

They told us there'd be eggs for breakfast, but there was just bacon without eggs. There was plenty of grousing about that too.

In the equipment hut I heard somebody say, "Today I'm catching up on my sack time." Some other gunner said, "I slept most of the way to Augsburg yesterday." Nobody said anything about the Luftwaffe. Leipzig is in there deep. . . .

We had an easy ride in. I didn't feel sleepy, I just felt dazed. There was a soft fuzz over a thin solid overcast, but inside Germany the clouds broke up. . . . The ground showed pale green through the holes.

"We're way back," Green [the pilot] said. The lead and high groups of our wing looked nice. But our group, the low, was way back and below. Our wing was the tail end, with most of the Eighth up ahead. . . .

There was death all over the sky, the quiet threat of death, the anesthesia of cold sunlight filled the cockpit. . . . The lead and high groups were already far above us. We were back there alone. We never caught up after that.

"I don't like this," Green said. "Tuck it in," somebody said over the radio. "Bandits [German fighters] in the target area." I was tense and drawn taut. The sky was cold and beautifully aloof. . . .

I saw some black puffs and a couple of bright bursts. We're in the flak already, I thought.

Then the guns opened up. Every gun on the ship opened up. A black Focke-Wulf slid under our wing, and rolled over low. I flipped over to interphone and fear was hot in my throat and cold in my stomach.

"Here they come." It was Mock [the tail gunner], cool and easy, like in church. Then his guns fired steadily. The air was nothing but black polka dots and firecrackers from the 20-millimeters.

"Keep your eye on 'em. . . . Keep 'em out there. . . ." It was Mock and Bossert [the ball turret gunner]. "Got the one at seven." Bossert or Mock. Steady.

They came through again, coming through from the tail. I saw two Forts blow up out at four o'clock. Some other group.

A trio of gray ones whipped past under the wing and rolled away at two o'clock. Black crosses on gray wings. ME-109s.

A night-fighter Focke-Wulf moved up almost in formation with us, right outside the window, throwing 20-millimeters into somebody up ahead. Somebody powdered him.

One came around at ten o'clock and the nose guns opened up on him. He rolled over and fell away; maybe there was smoke.

The instruments were fine. Green looked okay. My breath was in short gasps. "Better give me everything," Green said. Steady voice. I jacked up the RPMs to the hilt.

They were queuing up again back at four and six and eight o'clock. A hundred of them —maybe two hundred—getting set to come through again, fifteen or twenty abreast.

I looked up at the wing ship. The whole stabilizer was gone. I could see blue sky through there. But the rudder still worked —still flapped—then his wing flared up. He fell off to the right. He was gone. Green slid us in under the lead squadron. . . .

"Here they come!"

"Four o'clock level."

"Take that one at six."

All the guns were going again. There wasn't any hope at all—just waiting for it—just sitting there hunched up—jerking around to check the right side—jerking back to check the instruments—everything okay—just waiting for it.

They came through six times, I guess— maybe five—maybe seven—queuing up back there, coming in, throwing those shells in there. We were hit.

The whole low squadron was gone—blown up—burned out—shot to hell. One guy got out of that. . . . The lead squadron was okay.

We snuggled up almost under somebody's tail guns. They were firing steadily. The shell cases were dropping down and going through the cowling—smashing against the plexiglass —chipping away at the windshields—coming steady. Then his guns must have burned out.

There were a few P-51s back there. Four against a hundred—maybe eight. "Don't shoot that 51." Mock again, cool.

I punched the wheel forward. A burning plane was nosing over us. Green nodded, kept on flying. The guns were going—not all of them anymore—some of them were out.

And then it was over. They went away. We closed up and dropped our bombs. . . . We turned off the target—waiting for them— knowing they'd be back—waiting for them. . . .

I flicked back to the radio. No bandits called off. . . . I reached over and touched Green. What a guy. Then I felt the control column. Good airplane—still flying—still living. . . .

From the day you first get in a B-17 they say formation flying is the secret. They tell you over and over. Keep those planes tucked in and you'll come home. The ride home was easy. They never came back. . . .

When we got away from the Continent we began to come apart. Green took off his oxygen mask. There weren't any words, but we tried to say them. . . . Bradley came down out of the turret. His face was nothing but teeth. I mussed up his hair, and he beat on me. . . .

The clouds were under us again, almost solid, and then I saw a beach through a hole —white sand and England. There was never anywhere as beautiful as that. We were home.

Green made a sweet landing. We opened up the side windows and looked around. Everything looked different. There was too much light, too much green, just too much. We were home. . . .

Green swung around into place, and I cut the engines. We were home. . . .

A 20-millimeter had hit our wing. It blew up inside—blew away part of the top of number two gas tank—blew hell out of everything inside there. . . .

We didn't even lose any gas. We didn't even blow up. I stood back by the tail and looked at the hole. I could feel the ground, and I wanted to take my shoes off. Every time I breathed, I knew it. . . .

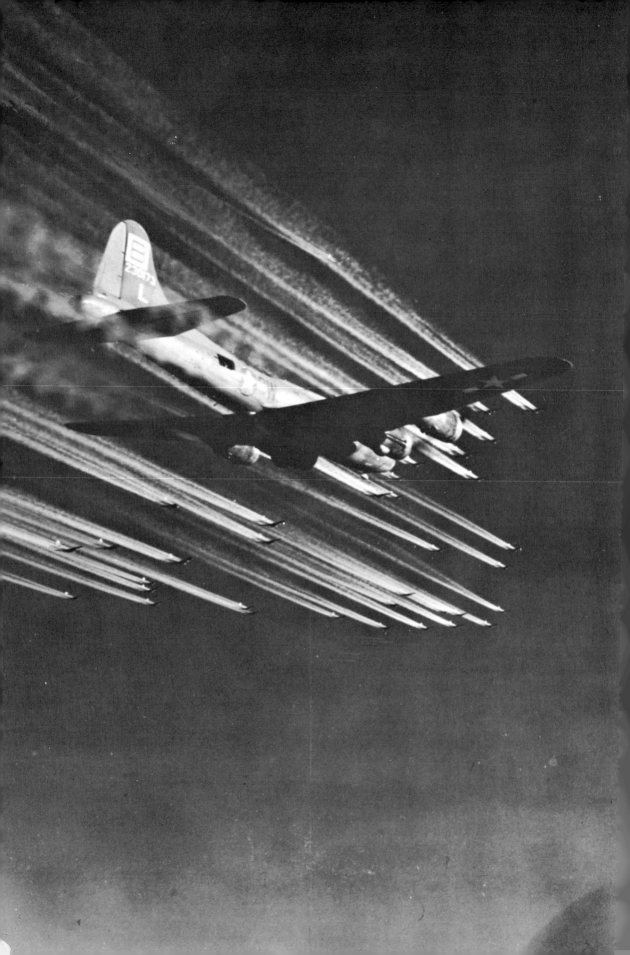

7

VICTORY IN THE AIR

" A clear dawn has a new clarion," an Englishman wrote in 1944, "—the deep and throbbing roar of hundreds of planes, outward bound. . . . Sometimes they look white and as graceful as gulls against the blue; at others they look black and sinister as they come and go between the clouds. But the impressive thing is the numbers. . . . As their roar fades with them another rises until things on the kitchen mantleshelf tinkle and rattle as they catch the vibration. Up over the beechwoods on the hill the leading formation of a second wave of heavies appears, followed by others and still others. . . . They have an appointment abroad, and they're keeping it."

This armada of American bombers the Englishman marveled at did indeed have an appointment—an appointment to smash Hitler's war machine. When the German dictator boasted that he had turned conquered Europe into a fortress, President Franklin Roosevelt remarked

Feathery contrails mark the passage of U.S. B-17s attacking Nazi Germany in 1944. The Allied air offensive hit full stride after D-Day; of the nearly 2,700,000 tons of bombs dropped on Hitler's empire, three-quarters of them fell in the final ten months of the war.

that Hitler forgot to put a roof on his fortress. Day and night American and British bombers pounded the enemy; then, on June 6, 1944, ground forces broke into Hitler's fortress by landing in France.

A chief task of the airmen in the summer of 1944 was the tactical support of Allied ground forces. Heavy bombers helped the armies in the beachhead by a tactic known as "carpet bombing"—that is, pulverizing the enemy defense line with an enormous concentration of high explosives. A German general said that after such an attack his position was as desolate as the landscape of the moon.

In July American tank forces burst free and rolled across France. The Luftwaffe was seldom seen. In August an entire German field army was pinched between the Americans on one side and the British and Canadians on the other. Within this pocket the fleeing enemy columns were slaughtered from the air.

The leaders of the air offensive were jubilant. They surveyed their vast strength—1,100 RAF bombers; 3,300 U.S. B-17s and B-24s of the

Eighth and Fifteenth air forces; and thousands of fighters, medium bombers, and fighter-bombers—and they thought that the war in Europe might be over by Christmas.

Roads cluttered with burned-out German tanks and trucks or railroad bridges in ruins offered grim proof of the force of tactical air power. It was up to the strategic bombers to see that the German war economy could not resupply and rebuild the Nazi armies now on the defensive in France, Italy, and Russia.

In the air, Luftwaffe defenses against daylight bombing had been beaten down. The night fighter defenses, too, were faltering. But another, less favorable fact was also clear: the RAF's nighttime area bombing was not having the effects expected of it.

Area bombing, as a British historian has written, worked "on the principle that in order to destroy anything it is necessary to destroy everything." Sir Arthur Harris—better known as "Bomber" Harris—ran his RAF Bomber Command with fierce, stubborn dedication to this principle. He reported that his planes were devastating the Third Reich at the rate of two and half cities a month. Yet neither the German economy nor the German people had collapsed under this murderous attack.

Thousands upon thousands of men, women, and children were killed and maimed, but the reaction of the survivors was just about the same as the reaction of England's civilians during the Blitz early in the war: they only worked harder to turn out weapons. Some method other than the wholesale destruction of cities had to be found if strategic bombing were to shorten the war.

Even before D-Day, the AAF's General Spaatz had strongly urged that both British and American bombers concentrate on one target—Germany's oil supply. Spaatz argued that oil and gasoline were essential to nearly every part of Hitler's war machine. But he was overruled by the Allied supreme command; knocking out the enemy transportation system appeared to be a better way to support the invasion forces.

Nevertheless, Spaatz managed to find the planes for a few oil raids before D-Day. Repeated attacks by the Fifteenth Air Force caused severe damage to Ploesti's refineries. The Eighth Air Force hit hard at plants in Germany that manufactured synthetic oil from coal. Then, after D-Day, and over the objections of Bomber Harris, Spaatz's policy was officially adopted. German oil production was put at the top of the target list.

As the attacks on refineries and synthetic plants mounted, Nazi leaders fell into deep gloom. Albert Speer, the skillful director of German war production, admitted after the war that such attacks "had been a nightmare to us." Speer could move ball bearing factories to safer locations far from Schweinfurt, or set up fighter

Generals Spaatz (left) and Doolittle question a crew just back from raiding Nazi oil plants. Spaatz headed the U.S. strategic bombing campaign; Doolittle took over the Eighth Air Force in late 1943.

plane assembly lines in caves or under thick concrete roofs, but there was little he could do about oil—refineries and synthetic plants were too big and too complex to move.

By July 1, 1944, German oil production was cut in half. In August the Russian army captured the Ploesti refineries, eliminating Hitler's largest supply of natural oil. By September oil output was down by more than 75 per cent. On the fighting fronts German tanks had to be towed to battle, and hundreds of them were abandoned because their fuel tanks were empty. Trucks gave way to horse-drawn wagons. There were fewer and fewer Luftwaffe sorties, and the training period of German pilots was cut to the bone to conserve precious aviation gasoline.

Some military historians argue that this oil offensive should have been started much earlier. Yet until the spring of 1944 the German Air Force dominated the air over Europe. The Luftwaffe would have reacted as viciously to an attack on oil as it did to the attacks on Schweinfurt's ball bearings or Regensburg's aircraft factories. The Americans had to achieve mastery of the air before they could achieve really effective precision bombing, regardless of the target.

It is true that the oil campaign might have been started in earnest before D-Day rather than afterward. At the time, however, it seemed to

General Eisenhower and some of his air advisers that the heavy bombers would be needed in the pre-invasion assault on German supply lines in France. Seeing the invading troops thrown back into the sea would have been a terrible price for Eisenhower to pay for guessing wrong.

At any rate, the oil campaign was succeeding brilliantly by fall. Then came the winter bad weather. Precision attacks became harder and harder to carry out, and oil production climbed slowly. The Americans tried to bomb through the clouds by radar, but this was no more successful than it had been the previous winter.

The Luftwaffe also began to show signs of life. Carefully hoarding gasoline, the fighters occasionally tried to stop the bombers. The German fighter pilots might be badly trained now and inexperienced, but they showed no lack of courage. The fighting was savage, and many bombers went down.

The vast majority of airmen who managed to parachute safely from crippled bombers sat out the war in German prison camps. Yet a number of them showed remarkable ingenuity in escaping imprisonment.

One man, bailing out of a burning B-17, floated down into the back-yard garden of a house in a Belgian village.

A spectacular mushroom-shaped cloud of smoke boils up from the German synthetic oil plant at Merseburg. At top right is a B-17 of the attacking force. One of the many U.S. raids on Merseburg in 1944 earned an extra dividend by wrecking a laboratory where scientists sought to develop an atomic bomb.

Almost immediately a German soldier on a motorcycle braked to a stop in front of the house and dashed around to the garden. No sooner had he disappeared than the U.S. flier ran out the front door, leaped on the German's motorcycle, and roared away to a safe hiding place.

Sergeant Nick Asvestos, a waist gunner, was captured the moment he landed. When he was pushed into the back of a waiting German staff car, he kept right on going out the other door. Amidst a barrage of shots he sprinted into a warehouse across the street, ducked out the rear door, and hid in a haystack. Eventually he made good his escape.

Even when they got their captives into prison camps, the Germans could never be sure they would stay there. An RAF airman, who spoke fluent German, made himself a Nazi officer's uniform with the aid of dye, shoe polish, tinfoil, and cardboard. One evening he strolled unchallenged out the main gate of the camp—but not before stopping to bawl out the sentry for giving him a sloppy salute.

Any number of escapes were made from prison camps by digging tunnels, but the challenge of walking out the main gate seemed to fascinate many Allied fliers. One man managed to obtain civilian clothes and a wheelbarrow, which he filled with bricks and sand. Thinking he was a civilian laborer, the guards obligingly opened the gate for him. He pushed his trusty wheelbarrow out of Nazi Germany, across France, and into neutral Spain.

Three U.S. airmen used a very different device—a reel of measuring tape—to make their escape. With two of them handling the tape and the third jotting down figures in a notebook, they measured their way right out the gate. They too made it to Spain. Whenever a German soldier or a policeman approached, they got out their tape and managed to look very official by measuring whatever was handy—poles, buildings, even curbs.

While such ingenious fliers matched wits with their captors on the ground, the war in the air continued without pause. One of the best reporters of the conflict was Bert Stiles, the young AAF officer whose account of the fighting over Leipzig appears on pages 120–121.

When he finished his combat tour as a B-17 copilot, Stiles learned to fly a Mustang, and in the fall of 1944 he wrote a magazine article about a mission he flew. Nothing very much happened to him—there were no spectacular dogfights with the Luftwaffe, for example—but his account reveals that the average fighter pilot on the average mission over Germany was far too busy being confused and nerv-

A British Tempest is shown in hot pursuit of a German V-1 "buzz bomb" (top right). Antiaircraft guns and fighters took a high toll of these jet-propelled weapons aimed at London. One RAF fighter pilot tried a novel tactic: he flew alongside a V-1 and flipped it over with his wingtip, upsetting its guidance system and causing it to crash.

ous to have much time left for heroics.

Lieutenant Stiles' flight of P-51s took off from a soggy English airfield and very nearly collided with a British bomber in a heavy overcast. "The clouds broke up when we hit the coast and we went up," Stiles wrote. "There were strings of '51s and '47s in back of us and on the sides and probably up ahead. . . .

"Somebody called in [on the radio] two planes up at two o'clock high. Somebody else called in four planes at two-thirty high.

"I saw them. They were coming right for us. I flicked up all the switches and got ready to drop my tanks and turn into them shooting. In two seconds I'll break, I decided. I shook with anticipation. I guess it was that.

"'Little fat friends,' somebody sang out. 'They're Jugs,' somebody else said in a relieved voice. P-47s, he meant. They swung off maybe a mile out, showing that big slice-of-orange wing and went off to look for something else. There was sweat on my hands and sweat on my legs and everywhere else.

"We were fanned out in battle formation. We were looking around. We were ready for the Luftwaffe. 'Bogies at nine o'clock,' somebody called in. Bogies are unknowns. Somebody else called them a little louder. 'They're 109s.' I flicked the switches on again.

"'Drop tanks in fifteen seconds, White Flight.' That was us. I let mine go in about three and was tied for last.

"We went into a screaming turn to the right. I . . . gave it full throttle. There were '51s all over the sky in a big swirl. I kept swiveling around— '51s on my tail—'51s at every hour on the clock. 'We turned the wrong way,' somebody said."

The Mustang pilots formed up again and hurried on. They saw no more enemy planes, but they did spot a number of oil tank cars on a railroad in a German village and went down to treetop level.

"We went round and round," Stiles continued. "There were enough '51s to shoot up ten towns that size. Somebody got the engines on the first pass. There were two trains, and we shot the hell out of them. . . . Then somebody went in. The whole works blew when he hit the ground, and his engine went shooting up over a little hill into the trees."

The Mustangs started home: "France was pretty. We let down to get under the front of clouds coming up. I did three rolls going down. Four hundred thousand men were moving up along a line from the Dutch coast to Switzerland. A couple of trains were lying back there, dead and smashed. A little village was shot up and scared and still there.

These pictures illustrate the crippling effects of Allied tactical attacks on German forces. Ogden Pleissner's painting at top shows a P-51 buzzing tanks in France knocked out by fighter-bombers. The battered V-2 rocket in Julian Stafford-Baker's painting (left) was on its way by train to a launching site when a British pilot spotted it.

131

Late in the war, the Germans tried to re-
gain control of the air over Europe with an
array of very high performance planes powered by jet or rocket engines. But because
of bumbling by high officials, the usual delays in perfecting any new weapons, and the
Allied bombing of the German war economy,
they came too late to help the Luftwaffe.

*Above: A test pilot enters a rocket-powered
Viper interceptor and roars off. The wooden
Viper was to carry enough fuel to launch one
attack; then the pilot would bail out. It
killed every test pilot who tried to fly it.*

*Below: The Arado 234 was the world's first
jet bomber. A number of twin-engine models
saw action, but only nineteen of the very
fast (534 miles per hour) four-engine type
shown had been built when the war ended.*

The one jet the Germans produced in any numbers was the Messerschmitt 262. Mustang escort fighters could seldom catch the ME-262s in the air, so they used their superior numbers and range to ambush them as they landed or took off. The Luftwaffe was able to equip only a few fighter squadrons with jets. Their best day was March 18, 1945, when 1,250 U.S. bombers hit Berlin. ME-262s shot down most of the 24 bombers and five P-51s lost in the raid.

The black sheep of the flock of German jets and rockets was the Heinkel Volksjäger, or "People's Fighter." This single-engine jet was simply designed and made partly of wood so as to be cheaply and quickly mass-produced. It was to be flown in a kind of Nazi last stand by teenage boys given a bare minimum of flight training. A total of 162 Volksjägers were built, but performance was bad and the outlandish pilot-program collapsed. None saw combat.

With a top speed of close to 600 miles per hour, plus a phenomenal climbing ability that took it to 30,000 feet in less than three minutes, the Messerschmitt 163 Komet was the hottest airplane of the war. Its rocket engine gulped so much fuel, however, that the pilot had only some three minutes left after his climb in which to attack; then he glided down to a landing. The few Komets produced were used to defend vital German synthetic oil plants.

"I sat still, then I did another roll, then I looked down at the soft green world. There wasn't any sense to it all.

"This is war, I thought. This is war in the air."

A short time later Bert Stiles was shot down and killed over Germany. That, too, was war in the air.

With the coming of winter, the optimism in the Allied camp evaporated. On both western and eastern fronts the Allied ground forces bogged down as Nazi resistance stiffened. The Luftwaffe continued its occasional stiff opposition. Worst of all, it seemed as if German scientists and airplane designers had no end of new weapons up their sleeves.

One of the first such weapons, a redesigned Focke-Wulf 190, had appeared by 1944. Mounting a more powerful engine, this interceptor was a worthy opponent for American escort fighters. Fortunately for the Allied fliers, the lack of experienced pilots and the shortage of gasoline, plus the stubborn refusal of Luftwaffe leaders to clear the assembly lines of the outdated ME-109, took the sting out of the new Focke-Wulf.

The V-1 and V-2 were true secret weapons. The jet-propelled V-1 "buzz bombs" caused a great deal of damage to English cities, but at least they could be brought down by antiaircraft fire or fast fighters. Then came the V-2, the first ballistic guided missile. This 14-ton rocket soared high into space, then plummeted downward toward its target at a speed of almost

Artist John McCoy witnessed this scene in April, 1945. An ME-262, one jet engine smoking after an attack on another bomber group, streaked through McCoy's B-24 group with a pair of Mustangs on its tail. The crippled jet could not shake the P-51s and was shot down.

Attackers and defenders continued to trade blows right to the end of the war. The B-17 above limped back to England after a direct hit by a flak shell killed two of its crew. The late-model FW-190 below was shot down in the final week of the war. Its wooden propeller is mute evidence of the effect of bombing on German industry.

1,800 miles per hour. There was no defense against it. All that could be done was to try to bomb out the factories that built it, or capture its launching sites.

Both the V-1 and the V-2 were actually just what Hitler called them—vengeance weapons. They might destroy large numbers of British homes and kill large numbers of British civilians, but they had no effect on the course of the war. They came too late for that.

Yet the Germans did develop one weapon that might well have overturned the whole Allied strategic bombing campaign. This was a jet-propelled fighter plane, the Messerschmitt 262. That it did not is largely due to the bullheadedness of Adolf Hitler and the timidity of Hermann Goering.

The ME-262 was powered by a pair of turbojet engines, one slung under each wing. The principle of the turbojet is basically simple: air is drawn into the engine, compressed, heated, mixed with fuel, and ignited. The resulting explosive thrust drives the plane forward. The Germans had taken a big head start in jet propulsion—they were the first to fly a jet, in 1939—but the Nazi leaders' strange decision in 1940 to pay little heed to experimental projects caused the development of the ME-262 to lag badly.

Messerschmitt engineers, however, were not ready to drop the radical design completely. They went ahead to try and solve the thorny technical problems of making an effective warplane out of the jet. One such problem, for example, was to develop metals to withstand the terrific heat generated in the engines. Finally they had the ME-262 ready for production in May of 1943—at the time when the Eighth Air Force was still struggling to launch as many as 200 heavy bombers against Germany.

This sleek fighter mounted four powerful cannon in the nose. Test pilots found it fast-climbing, maneuverable, and easy to fly. And with its top speed of 540 miles per hour, there was not a propeller-driven plane in all the world that could come anywhere near catching it.

German pilots were understandably enthusiastic; even Goering was excited. But Hitler was not. The dictator threw their reports on the floor. "I want bombers, bombers, bombers!" he bellowed. "Your fighters are no damned good!" Not until six months later would he even consent to watch a test flight. Then he had to admit he was impressed; he ordered the fighter to be converted into a bomber.

Luftwaffe officers were flabbergasted. The jet lacked the range and the weight-carrying ability to be an effective bomber. Badgered by his officers, Goering tried to change Hitler's mind. But the one-time hero of the Third Reich had lost his prestige and his influence by this stage of the war. Goering admitted that each time he nerved himself to stand up to the Fuehrer, "when I come face

These water colors show some of the devastation in Berlin caused by strategic bombing. At the top of this page is a technical school, and below it is the headquarters of the dreaded Nazi secret police.

The German Propaganda Ministry (top) and Hermann Goering's Air Ministry (below) were gutted by the Allied bombers. Julian Stafford-Baker did these paintings soon after Germany's collapse.

to face with him my heart sinks into my boots."

The result of all this fumbling was that the ME-262—as well as several other jets and rocket-powered fighters —had no bearing whatever on the war situation. They might have kept control of the air for the Luftwaffe in 1944, or, at the very least, severely hampered the bomber offensive. Instead, the jets did not appear in any numbers until just a few months before the war's end. By then, the outcome was no longer in doubt.

Even so, these new weapons greatly disturbed Allied leaders. In the fall of 1944 an occasional ME-262 was seen, surging away from pursuing Mustangs as if the high-performance American fighters were chained to posts. Then came the German army's surprising December counterattack through Belgium toward the chief Allied supply depot at Antwerp—the Battle of the Bulge.

It is known now that the rockets, the jet fighters, and the ill-fated Bulge attack were all last-ditch moves of a dying nation. The oil offensive and the air attacks on transportation begun in the fall of 1944 had severed the arteries of Germany's industrial heart. These counterattacks were no more than the death rattles of Adolf Hitler's Thousand Year Reich.

As clear as this is now, it was not quite so clear then. In part because of this uneasiness, a new mood gripped the Allied high command. The war could not end, they felt, until Nazi Germany was so devastated that its will to resist, secret weapons or no secret weapons, was broken.

From the beginning of the war American air leaders had stubbornly refused to follow any bomber strategy that made the German people the number one target. The whole idea behind daylight precision bombing was to destroy key industrial targets that would cripple Hitler's war economy without wholesale slaughter of civilians. "We should never allow the history of this war to convict us of throwing the strategic bomber at the man in the street," insisted General Eaker. Mistakes were made, of course. But on the whole, U.S. strategists had stuck to their policy, accepting terrible losses in men and planes to do it.

But now, as 1944 became 1945, a change took place. Allied armies in the west were poised to make the final thrust into Germany. From the east the masses of the Russian army began to close in. As the Axis domain shrank, the U.S. bombers stepped up mass attacks. In destroying such targets as railroad yards, the raiders also destroyed acre after acre of public buildings and homes. Daylight precision bombing was becoming daylight area bombing.

The most tragic result of this tendency was the destruction of Dresden. This historic town in eastern Germany, "a fairy-tale city of spires and cobbled streets," as one writer described it, had hardly been touched by the war until February of 1945.

The heavy and repeated air attacks on German transportation brought rail traffic almost to a standstill by 1945. Allied troops advancing into Germany came upon sights like the jackknifed locomotive at left. The picture below, showing the shattered rail yards at Leipzig, was taken from a low-flying U.S. fighter in May, 1945.

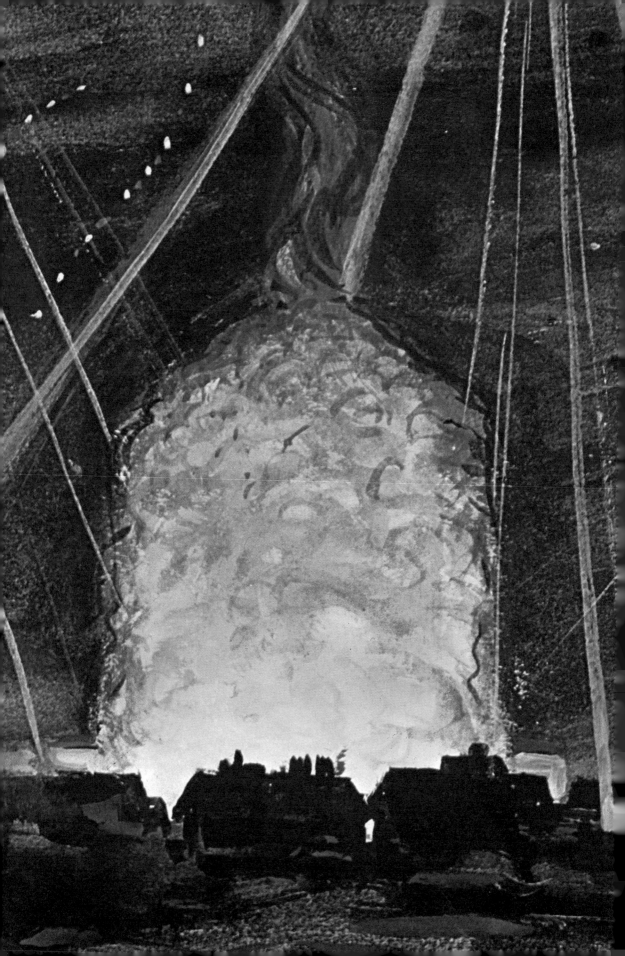

There had been no good reason to touch it, for it contained few factories of any importance to the Nazi war effort. Now it was jammed with hundreds of thousands of refugees fleeing from the advancing Russians.

In an apparent attempt to show the Russians that Allied air power could lend a hand to the Red Army, Dresden was put at the top of the target list. In the space of fourteen hours, on February 13 and 14, two RAF night raids and one American daylight raid gutted Dresden from end to end.

A massive fire storm swept the ruins, creating a whirlwind so strong that it sucked victims into the inferno. The fires burned for a week. In scenes of unbelievable horror, an estimated 135,000 people died—about twice the number killed when the first atomic bomb was dropped on the Japanese city of Hiroshima the following August. A German who watched the bombing wrote, "He who no longer knows how to cry learns to cry again at the end of Dresden."

The bombing grew even heavier as victory came into sight. German transportation systems were completely paralyzed. War production ground to a halt. Fighter pilots fat-

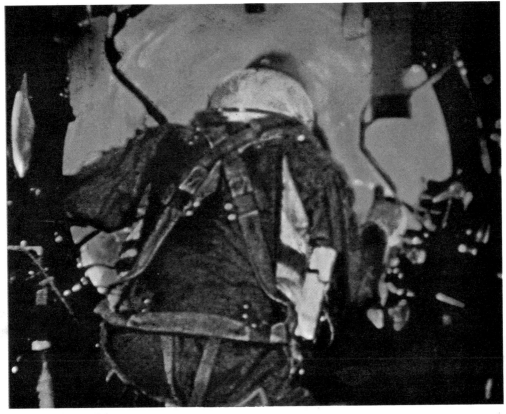

The German painting at left shows a fire storm created in Berlin by the RAF. Above, a British bombardier aims at Dresden. Light from the burning city is reflected in the plexiglass nose of the bomber.

tened their scores by strafing rows of Luftwaffe fighters, their gas tanks empty, parked neatly on airfields.

And men continued to die in the air. When Luftwaffe pilots scavenged enough gasoline they did not hesitate to attack the raiders and their fighter escorts. A group of the greatest surviving fighter aces of the Luftwaffe formed a squadron of ME-262 jets and struck hard at the U.S. bombers.

It seems doubtful that these men were any longer fighting for Adolf Hitler. What they were battling was the force laying waste their homeland, house by house and brick by brick.

There is perhaps another reason for their fight against odds—the airman's pride. This was the same pride shown by the RAF fighter pilots in the Battle of Britain, and by the American bomber crews who never once turned back because of combat losses even in such bloody battles as Ploesti or Regensburg or Schweinfurt or Berlin. Airmen of both sides were proud of their skills, proud of their privilege, as one RAF pilot said, of killing cleanly if they had to kill at all.

The killing ended at last on May 7, 1945, when the remnants of Germany's armed forces surrendered. Adolf Hitler had already killed himself. (A year and a half later Hermann Goering, too, died by his own hand, only hours before he was to be hanged as a war criminal.) The Allied victory was complete; Germany lay in ruins.

Exactly how large a share of the victory can be credited to the American daylight bombing campaign will never be known precisely. It took more than a year and a half to perfect the strategy and to clear a path for it. Only after the airmen wrested control of European skies from the Luftwaffe (to the great benefit of Allied ground forces), did daylight raids finally begin to yield dividends. By the summer of 1944, when air attacks on German oil production and transportation intensified, American bombers, by themselves, were playing a decisive part in the march to victory.

That achievement stands as the epitaph of the 79,265 American fliers killed in action in the air war over Europe. As for the enemy, a German writer admitted sadly that his own nation, in taking up the sword to conquer the world, had "summoned up those bands of furies which raced across the German skies."

Furious indeed had been the air war against Hitler's Germany; furious and successful.

A statue appears to grieve over the ruins of Dresden, photographed three months after the RAF and the AAF combined to level it in February of 1945. A night assault by some 800 British bombers was followed up the next day by 316 Fortresses, escorted by Mustang fighters that strafed the city.
ERICH ANDRES, HAMBURG

OVERLEAF: *This is how the transportation center of Wesel, on the Rhine River in western Germany, looked after a month of concentrated bombing early in 1945. On April 16, having run out of targets to bomb, the Allied strategic air campaign against Germany was halted. Three weeks later the war ended.*
U.S. AIR FORCE

U.S. AIR FORCE

A battery of German 88-millimeter flak guns.

AMERICAN HERITAGE PUBLISHING CO., INC.

PRESIDENT JAMES PARTON

EDITORIAL DIRECTOR JOSEPH J. THORNDIKE, JR.

EDITOR, BOOK DIVISION RICHARD M. KETCHUM

ART DIRECTOR IRWIN GLUSKER

AMERICAN HERITAGE JUNIOR LIBRARY

MANAGING EDITOR RUSSELL BOURNE

ART DIRECTOR ELEANOR A. DYE

CHIEF PICTURE RESEARCHER JULIA POTTS GREHAN

PICTURE RESEARCHER MARY LEVERTY

COPY EDITOR BARBARA FISHER SHOR

EDITORIAL ASSISTANT NANCY SIMON

EDITORIAL ASSISTANT BETSY SANDERS

ACKNOWLEDGMENTS

The editors are indebted to the following individuals and institutions for their generous assistance in preparing this book:

Department of the Air Force—Lieutenant Colonel Gene Guerny, Mrs. Alice R. Martin, William H. Winder, Mrs. Frances Lewis

Department of the Army (Historical Properties Branch)—Mrs. Marian McNaughton

Maureen Green, London

The Imperial War Museum, London—Dr. Noble Frankland, W.P. Mayes, J.F. Golding

David Irving, London

Egon Krueger, Weiden, Oberpfalz, West Germany

Library of Congress, Washington—Virginia Daiker

John T. McCoy, Jr., New York

National Archives, Washington—Joe E. Thomas

Susanne Puddefoot, London

Richard M. Skinner, *Air Force/Space Digest*

The excerpt on pages 120–121 from *Serenade to the Big Bird*, by Bert Stiles (© 1947 by Mrs. Bert W. Stiles), is used by permission of the publisher, W.W. Norton and Company Inc. Beirne Lay's account of the Regensburg mission, quoted on pages 81–82, and Bert Stiles' account of a fighter mission, quoted on pages 131 and 134, appeared in wartime issues of *Air Force* magazine and are used by permission of the Air Force Association. Quotations from the diary of a German fighter pilot, on pages 52–53, 58, and 110–111, are from *I Flew for the Führer*, by Heinz Knoke, used by permission of the publisher, Holt, Rinehart and Winston, Inc. Victor Amato of Washington photographed many of the paintings. The photograph of the painting on page 142 is used through the courtesy of Time Inc.

FOR FURTHER READING

Baumbach, Werner, *The Life and Death of the Luftwaffe*. Coward-McCann, 1960.

Caidin, Martin, *Black Thursday* (The Schweinfurt raid, October 14, 1943). E. P. Dutton, 1960.

Clostermann, Pierre, *The Big Show*. Random House, 1957.

Craven, Frank W., and Cate, James L., *The Army Air Forces in World War II*, Vols. I–III. University of Chicago Press, 1948–1951.

Galland, Adolf, *The First and the Last*. Holt, 1954.

Godfrey, John T., *The Look of Eagles*. Random House, 1958.

Goldberg, Alfred, *A History of the United States Air Force, 1907–1957*. Van Nostrand, 1957.

Green, William, *Famous Fighters of the Second World War*, 2 vols. Doubleday, 1957.

Green, William, *Famous Bombers of the Second World War*, 2 vols. Doubleday, 1957.

Hine, Al, *D-Day, The Invasion of Europe*. American Heritage Junior Library, 1962.

Irving, David, *The Destruction of Dresden*, Holt, Rinehart & Winston, 1964.

Johnson, Robert S., *Thunderbolt*. Rinehart, 1958.

Knoke, Heinz, *I Flew for the Führer*. Holt, 1954.

Loosbrock, John F., and Skinner, Richard M., Editors, *The Wild Blue: The Story of American Airpower*. G. P. Putnam's Sons, 1961.

Manvell, Roger and Fraenkel, Heinrich, *Goering*. Simon & Schuster, 1962.

Middleton, Drew, *The Sky Suspended: The Story of the Battle of Britain*. David McKay, 1960.

Snyder, Louis L., *The War, A Concise History, 1939–1945*. Julian Messner, 1960.

Stewart, Carroll, and Dugan, James, *Ploesti*. Random House, 1962.

Stiles, Bert, *Serenade to the Big Bird*. W. W. Norton, 1952.

Sunderman, James F., Editor, *World War II in the Air: Europe*. Franklin Watts, 1963.

Wagner, Ray, *American Combat Planes*. Doubleday, 1960.

Webster, Charles, and Frankland, Noble, *The Strategic Air Offensive Against Germany, 1939–1945*, 4 vols. Her Majesty's Stationary Office, 1961.

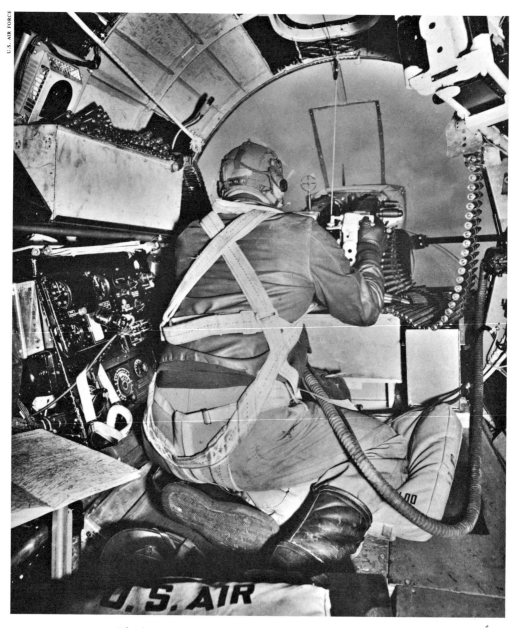

The bombardier of a Flying Fortress mans his guns.

Index

Bold face indicates pages on which illustrations appear